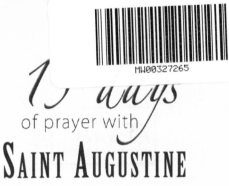

15 *days*
of prayer with

SAINT AUGUSTINE

15 days
of prayer/series

On a journey, it's good to have a guide. Even great saints took spiritual directors or confessors with them on their itineraries toward sanctity. Now you can be guided by the most influential spiritual figures of all time. The 15 Days of Prayer series introduces their deepest and most personal thoughts.

This popular series is perfect if you are looking for a gift, or if you want to be introduced to a particular guide and his or her spirituality. Each volume contains:

- ✿ A brief biography of the saint or spiritual leader
- ✿ A guide to creating a format for prayer or retreat
- ✿ Fifteen meditation sessions with focus points and reflection guides

15 days
of prayer with
SAINT AUGUSTINE

JAIME GARCÍA

NEW CITY PRESS
of the Focolare
Hyde Park, NY

Published in the United States by New City Press
202 Comforter Blvd., Hyde Park, NY 12538
www.newcitypress.com
©2013 Jaime Alvarez García (English Translation)

This book is a translation of *Prier 15 Jours Avec Saint Augustine, ou La Voix du Coeur*, published by Nouvelle Cité, 1995, Montrouge, France.

© Nouvelle Cité 1999
Used by permission. All rights reserved.

Cover design by Durva Correia

A catalog record is available from the Library of Congress.

ISBN 978-1-56548-489-4

Printed in the United States of America

Contents

How to Use
This Book

*A*n old Chinese proverb, or at least what I am able to recall of what is supposed to be an old Chinese proverb, goes something like this: "Even a journey of a thousand miles begins with a single step." When you think about it, the truth of the proverb is obvious. It is impossible to begin any project, let alone a journey, without taking the first step. I think it might also be true, although I cannot recall if another Chinese proverb says it, "that the first step is often the hardest." Or, as someone else once observed, "the distance between a thought and the corresponding action needed to implement the idea takes the most energy." I don't know who shared that perception with me but I am certain it was not an old Chinese master!

With this ancient proverbial wisdom, and the not-so-ancient wisdom of an unknown

7

contemporary sage still fresh, we move from proverbs to presumptions. How do these relate to the task before us?

I am presuming that if you are reading this introduction it is because you are contemplating a journey. My presumption is that you are preparing for a spiritual journey and that you have taken at least some of the first steps necessary to prepare for this journey. I also presume, and please excuse me if I am making too many presumptions, that in your preparation for the spiritual journey you have determined that you need a guide. From deep within the recesses of your deepest self, there was something that called you to consider Saint Augustine as a potential companion. If my presumptions are correct, may I congratulate you on this decision? I think you have made a wise choice, a choice that can be confirmed by yet another source of wisdom, the wisdom that comes from practical experience.

Even an informal poll of experienced travelers will reveal a common opinion; it is very difficult to travel alone. Some might observe that it is even foolish. Still others may be even stronger in their opinion and go so far as to insist that it is necessary to have a guide, especially when you are traveling into uncharted waters and into territory that you have not yet experienced. I am of the personal opinion that a traveling companion is welcome under all circumstances. The thought of traveling alone, to some exciting destination without someone to share the journey with does not capture my imagination or channel my enthusiasm. However, with that being noted, what is simply a matter of preference on the normal journey becomes a matter of necessity when a person embarks on a spiritual journey.

The spiritual journey, which can be the most challenging of all journeys, is experienced best with a guide, a companion, or at the very least, a friend in whom you have placed your trust. This observation is not a preference or an opinion but rather an established spiritual necessity. All of the great saints with whom I am familiar had a spiritual director or a confessor who journeyed with them. Admittedly, at times the saints might well have traveled far beyond the experience of their guide and companion but more often than not they would return to their director and reflect on their experience. Understood in this sense, the director and companion provided a valuable contribution and necessary resource. When I was learning how to pray (a necessity for anyone who desires to be a full-time and public "religious person"), the community of men that I belong to gave me a great gift. Between my second and third year in college, I was given a one-year sabbatical, with all expenses paid and all of my personal needs met. This period of time was called novitiate. I was officially designated as a novice, a beginner in the spiritual journey, and I was assigned a "master," a person who was willing to lead me. In addition to the master, I was provided with every imaginable book and any other resource that I could possibly need. Even with all that I was provided, I did not learn how to pray because of the books and the unlimited resources, rather it was the master, the companion who was the key to the experience.

One day, after about three months of reading, of quiet and solitude, and of practicing all of the methods and descriptions of prayer that were available to me, the master called. "Put away the books, forget the method, and just listen." We went into a room, became quiet, and tried to recall the presence of God, and then, the master simply prayed out loud and permitted me to listen to his prayer. As he prayed, he revealed his hopes, his dreams, his struggles, his successes, and most of all, his relationship with God. I discovered as I listened that his prayer was deeply intimate but most of all it was self-revealing. As I learned about him, I was led through his life experience to the place where God dwells. At that moment I was able to understand a little bit about what I was supposed to do if I really wanted to pray.

The dynamic of what happened when the master called, invited me to listen, and then revealed his innermost self to me as he communicated with God in prayer, was important. It wasn't so much that the master was trying to reveal to me what needed to be said; he was not inviting me to pray with the same words that he used, but rather that he was trying to bring me to that place within myself where prayer becomes possible. That place, a place of intimacy and of self-awareness, was a necessary stop on the journey and it was a place that I needed to be led to. I could not have easily discovered it on my own.

The purpose of the volume that you hold in your hand is to lead you, over a period of fifteen days or, maybe more realistically, fifteen prayer periods, to a place where prayer is possible. If you already have a regular experience and practice of prayer, perhaps this volume can help lead you to a deeper place, a more intimate relationship with the Lord.

It is important to note that the purpose of this book is not to lead you to a better relationship with Saint Augustine, your spiritual companion. Although your companion will invite you to share some of his deepest and most intimate thoughts, your companion is doing so only to bring you to that place where God dwells. After all, the true measurement of all companions for the journey is that they bring you to the place where you need to be, and then they step back, out of the picture. A guide who brings you to the desired destination and then sticks around is a very unwelcome guest!

Many times I have found myself attracted to a particular idea or method for accomplishing a task, only to discover that what seemed to be inviting and helpful possessed too many details. All of my energy went to the mastery of the details and I soon lost my enthusiasm. In each instance, the book that seemed so promising ended up on my bookshelf, gathering dust. I can assure you, it is not our intention that this book end up in your bookcase, filled with promise, but unable to deliver.

There are three simple rules that need to be followed in order to use this book with a measure of satisfaction.

Place: It is important that you choose a place for reading that provides the necessary atmosphere for reflection and that does not allow for too many distractions. Whatever place you choose needs to be comfortable, have the necessary lighting, and, finally, have a sense of "welcoming" about it. You need to be able to look forward to the experience of the journey. Don't travel steerage if you know you will be more comfortable in first class and if the choice is realistic for you. On the other hand, if first class is a distraction and you feel more comfortable and more yourself in steerage, then it is in steerage that you belong.

My favorite place is an overstuffed and comfortable chair in my bedroom. There is a light over my shoulder, and the chair reclines if I feel a need to recline. Once in a while, I get lucky and the sun comes through my window and bathes the entire room in light. I have other options and other places that are available to me but this is the place that I prefer.

Time: Choose a time during the day when you are most alert and when you are most receptive to reflection, meditation, and prayer. The time that you choose is an essential component. If you are a morning person, for example, you should choose a time that is in the morning. If you are more alert in the afternoon, choose an afternoon time slot; and if evening is your preference, then by all means choose the evening. Try to avoid "peak" periods in your daily routine when you know that you might be disturbed. The time that you choose needs to be your time and needs to work for you.

It is also important that you choose how much time you will spend with your companion each day. For some it will be possible to set aside enough time in order to read and reflect on all the material that is offered for a given day. For others, it might not be possible to devote one time to the suggested material for the day, so the prayer period may need to be extended for two, three, or even more sessions. It is not important how long it takes you; it is only important that it works for you and that you remain committed to that which is possible.

For myself I have found that fifteen minutes in the early morning, while I am still in my robe and pajamas and before my morning coffee, and even before I prepare myself for the day, is the best time. No one expects to see me or to interact with me because I have not yet "announced" the fact that I am awake or even on the move. However, once someone hears me in the bathroom, then my window of opportunity is gone. It is therefore important to me that I use the time that I have identified when it is available to me.

Freedom: It may seem strange to suggest that freedom is the third necessary ingredient, but I have discovered that it is most important. By freedom I understand a certain "stance toward life," a "permission to be myself and to be gentle and understanding of who I am." I am constantly amazed at how the human person so easily sets himself or herself up for disappointment and perceived failure. We so easily make judgments about ourselves and our actions and our choices, and very often those judgments are negative, and not at all helpful.

For instance, what does it really matter if I have chosen a place and a time, and I have missed both the place and the time for three days in a row? What does it matter if I have chosen, in that twilight time before I am completely awake and still a little sleepy, to roll over and to sleep for fifteen minutes more? Does it mean that I am not serious about the journey, that I really don't want to pray, that I am just fooling myself when I say that my prayer time is important to me? Perhaps, but I prefer to believe that it simply means that I am tired and I just wanted a little more sleep. It doesn't mean anything more than that. However, if I make it mean more than that, then I can become discouraged, frustrated, and put myself into a state where I might more easily give up. "What's the use? I might as well forget all about it."

The same sense of freedom applies to the reading and the praying of this text. If I do not find the introduction to each day helpful, I don't need to read it. If I find the questions for reflection at the end of the appointed day repetitive, then I should choose to close the book and go my own way. Even if I discover that the reflection offered for the day is not the one that I prefer and that the one for the next day seems more inviting, then by all means, go on to the one for the next day.

That's it! If you apply these simple rules to your journey you should receive the maximum benefit and you will soon find yourself at your destination. But be prepared to be surprised. If you have never been on a spiritual journey you should know that the "travel brochures" and the other descriptions that you might have heard are nothing compared to the real thing. There is so much more than you can imagine.

A final prayer of blessing suggests itself:

> Lord, catch me off guard today.
> Surprise me with some moment of
>   beauty or pain
> So that at least for the moment
> I may be startled into seeing that you
>   are here in all your splendor,
> Always and everywhere,
> Barely hidden,
> Beneath,
> Beyond,
> Within this life I breathe.

Frederick Buechner

Rev. Thomas M. Santa, CSsR
Liguori, Missouri

A Brief
Chronology of
Saint Augustine's Life

Saint Augustine was one of the most important philosophers and theologians of the
early Christian era. While he was the bishop of
Hippo, he was the leading figure in the North
African Church. He exerted a profound influence on the later development of thought and
culture for Western civilizations, and, more
than anyone else, delineated the problems and
formulated the ideas that have characterized
the Western tradition of Christian theology.
Many of his writings are considered classics
(he is reported to have left over five million
words in print); two of which are the most cel-
ebrated: his *Confessions* (semi-autobiographical
with elements of mysticism) and *City of God* (a
Christian view of history).

354–386:

November 13, 354: Augustine was born of a devout Christian mother, Monica, and a pagan father, Patricus (who converted and was baptized on his deathbed), at Thagaste (modern day Souk-Ahras, Algeria); they were of the "middle class," yet impoverished. His mother raised him as a Christian, but he was not baptized. It has been said that religion never held an importance for Augustine during his early years, but it did have a decisive hold on him. He studied in Carthage (in Latin, as that had become the language of Roman Africa), receiving a classical education, with a strong emphasis on philosophy and literature. He was trained in rhetoric, which was a prerequisite for a legal or political career, and became a teacher of rhetoric in Carthage, Rome, and finally, Milan. His philosophical studies concentrated mainly on the works of Plato, Cicero, Virgil, and, later, on Manichaeism for nine years (a religious cult from Persia that allowed him to reconcile his sensual side with his intellectual aspirations), which resulted in his virtual renunciation of Christianity for that period. He lived with a mistress for fifteen years, producing a son, Adeodatus (who would stay with Augustine until his premature death in late adolescence).

386–396:

After becoming tired of such a vague theology, in 386, in Milan, he underwent religious conversion, after much interior conflict, as seen in his *Confessions*, retired from his public position, and, after forty days of preparation before Easter, 387, was baptized by Ambrose, the bishop of Milan, who exerted great influence over Augustine. He found that he was at last able to give up his ambition for a public life and devote himself to a search for truth, which he equated with Christianity. His mother was also greatly influential in his conversion. Augustine soon decided to return to North Africa (in 388) with a small group of friends and establish a religious community which would seek to provide a monastic lifestyle in which they would pray and study Scripture. While awaiting their boat to return, Monica unexpectedly died. Augustine did return in 389, settling in Thagaste.

In 391, he was unexpectedly ordained to the priesthood (some say that he was forced into it by popular demand) in Hippo. Tears came to his eyes as they laid hands on him in the Church. He had often stated that these were tears of inadequacy. This brought a fundamental philosophical change to his life and his way of thinking; his attention became redirected from the philosophic Christianity that he had seen in Milan to the turbulent, popular Christianity he saw in North Africa. Accepting his fate, he retired to devote himself to the mastery of Scripture. By 393, his speaking talents were well recognized, and he was often asked to speak in the place of the Greek-speaking bishop. The bishop passed away in 395 and Augustine assumed the responsibility as bishop for the Church in Hippo and would single-handedly rule that region until his death in 430.

396–411:

The first fifteen years of his career as a bishop were marked by controversy — most notable were his conflicts with the Donatists (Christian separatists) and the Pelagianists (reformists stressing the freedom of the human will). In both of these controversies, Augustine opposed forces that set individual Christians apart from others on the grounds of either religious exclusivity or moral values.

It is said that there were three major battles that Augustine fought through his writing: the ecclesiastical struggle for the life of his community; a philosophical battle to Christianize the Roman culture; and a theological quarrel over the essentials of faith and salvation.

412–430:

Little is known specifically about this later period of Augustine's life.

What is known is that he fought decisive philosophical battles, lived many a controversy, was greatly respected, showed an intellectual brilliance unknown before his time, and was voraciously criticized.

Information indicates that he fell ill in 430 and died in the late summer as the Saxons were attacking the city of Hippo. The city was captured shortly afterwards.

Augustine was one of the architects of modern Christianity. He stressed that Christianity was not something external and visible, found in obedience to laws, but a matter of spirit, something that was inside people. He also stated that the Church had room for both sinners and saints, for the imperfections of those in whom God's grace was still at work, deeming the Church open to all. By bringing together the philosophical Christianity of his youth with the popular Christianity of his congregation in Hippo, he created a theology that has remained basic to Western Christianity, both Roman Catholic and Protestant, ever since that time.

He is a Doctor of the Church; called the Doctor of Grace. His feast day is August 28. He is the patron saint of brewers.

A listing of approximate dates for his most notable written works is as follows: *Confessions* (400); *The City of God* (413– 426); *Retractions* (428); epistles (386– 429); various treatises — *On Free Will* (388–95); *On Christian Doctrine* (397); *On Baptism* (400); *On the Trinity* (400–416); and *On Nature and Grace* (415).

Abbreviations Used in This Book

Conf	*Confessions*
Cont Faust Manich	*Against Faust, the Manichean*
De agone Christ	*The Christian Battle*
De cat rud	*The Catechism of the Ignorant*
De civ Dei	*The City of God*
De doct Christ	*The Christian Doctrine*
De ser Dmi in monte	*Commentary on the Lord's Sermon on the Mount*
De Trinit	*The Holy Trinity*
De vera rel	*The True Religion*
De virg	*The Virginity*
En in ps	*Sermons on the Psalms*
Ep	*Letters*
In Joh ep	*Treatises on the First Letter of Saint John*

In Joh ev	*Treatises on the Gospel of Saint John*
Reg	*Rule of Saint Augustine*
Ser	*Sermons*
Sol	*Soliloquies*

Introduction

Be God's refuge and he will be your refuge. May he abide in you and you in him
(En in ps 30, 2, 8).

*P*rayer is an intimate and profound dialogue with the Lord: we speak to God
like we are speaking with our best friend. In the
presence of God, Saint Augustine meditated,
questioned himself, and questioned God. Even
more than that, he addressed God like a child
addresses his mother: He said — "And I chatter with you" (Conf IX, 1,1). Therefore, we must
try to emulate Saint Augustine's prayer in the
light of friendship because, for him, prayer is a
friendship that speaks for itself: "Your prayer is
a conversation with God" (En in ps 85,7). But
for him, prayer is much more than a dialogue
using words; it is, above all, a dialogue of life.
In it, God gives himself to us and we give ourselves to God.

It is certain that Saint Augustine was trained for prayer by his mother, Saint Monica. Even as a small child, he prayed to God with all of his heart.

As a boy, I began to pray to you, my help and my refuge, and by invoking you, I broke the knots which bound my tongue. As a little child, with an ardor that was not small, I prayed to you that I might not be beaten at school (Conf I, 9,14).

It is of great interest to accompany Saint Augustine in his evolution in prayer, for the steps he took to enter into true prayer are our own steps. We meet ourselves in him. Saint Augustine is a true master of prayer: he prays and teaches us to pray.

It is certain that when we begin to pray, we are often taken with ourselves, by our needs, and we speak to God about ourselves. We ask him for things, even explanations about events that happen to us. That is the prayer of Saint Augustine as a child, the prayer of Saint Augustine in his conversion. At that time, we are too centered and concentrated upon ourselves and we seek to get God to serve us.

God wants a disinterested following, freely-given love, that is, pure love. He does not want to be loved because he gives something outside of himself, but because he gives of himself. One who invokes God in order to become rich does not invoke God; he invokes what he wants for himself. For to invoke is to call to oneself. When you say: God, give me wealth, you don't want God himself to come to you, you want the wealth to come to you. What you want to come to you is what you invoke. If, to the contrary, you invoke God, he will come to you himself and he will be your wealth. But, in reality, you want to have your treasure chest filled and your conscience empty. God doesn't fill treasure chests, but hearts (En in ps 52,8).

To pray and pray well, we must begin by detaching ourselves from ourselves and look only at God. Prayer is an expression of love. Where there is a lack of love, prayer is impossible. We learn to pray just as we learn to love. Prayer, true prayer, is completely oriented towards God. But to orient our desires towards God is the result of conversion. That is why we must never separate prayer from conversion. The conversion of Augustine was a conversion to prayer.

Saint Augustine lived his conversion, and in other respects, his prayer was a conversion to the welcome. From the time of his conversion, he never stopped listening to God through the Scriptures and in the events of his life. He would make his life a permanent meditation. If he dedicated so many hours to the study of Scripture, it was not to seek information or make a scientific study; it was to feel God who spoke to him, who addressed himself to him like a friend speaks to another friend.

Your prayer is a conversation with God. When you read, it is God who speaks to you; when you pray, it is with God you are speaking (En in ps 85,7).

For Saint Augustine, the entire problem with prayer would be to feel God's love for us. Prayer is the expression of a friendship; a friendship that expresses itself and that takes the form of a conversation. But our love with respect to God is not first. Love the one who, first of all, felt love. And God loved us first and gives us something to love. Prayer is the response to this love that God shows us.

And God speaks to us, God tells us of his love in the deepest part of our heart. In order to hear God, we must, then, enter into the heart. Interiority and contemplation are absolutely necessary in order to pray. Saint Augustine never stopped inviting us to enter into the heart, for it is there that Christ, the Master of the interior, speaks to us and teaches us.

Christ is inside of you, his dwelling is
there. Present him with your prayer, but
don't act as if he is far away. The wisdom of God is never far away.... Yes, it
is within the deepest part of yourself: let
your prayer flow before him and he will
hear (En in ps 141,4).

Yet, in order to pray, and pray well, we must
also know how to model our prayer on Jesus'
prayer, on the Our Father. The Our Father is
a prayer and a true school of prayer itself. The
requests that are formulated there are the light
which permits us to discern what we must ask
of God.

The Our Father then purifies our requests
and, at the same time, reveals to us what we are
and what we should be. In him, we discover
the truth about ourselves.

But to pray the Our Father well, which is the
model for all true prayer, we must be inhabited
by the Spirit of Jesus and pray as he prayed. Yet,
the Spirit of Jesus, the Holy Spirit, is the soul
of the Church, the soul of the entire Christian
community. If we then want to pray, we must
be moved by the Holy Spirit which we will be,
in so much as we are a part of the ecclesiastical
community.

One of the very first conditions for prayer is
the one that we need so that our relationships

are ones of quality: to know how to open our hearts to others and welcome them. The person who needs no one and lives his life enclosed on himself will listen to no one, even less to God.

It is certain that God asks us to pray endlessly. Prayer is the life of the soul. To stop praying is to stop loving and to stop living. However, to pray does not mean uninterrupted prayers, but to make the desire of our heart never anything other than desires that are oriented towards God. To pray is to desire God.

Saint Augustine prays and teaches us to pray. The writings in this book are not and do not presuppose to be a complete and systematic exposé of Saint Augustine's thoughts about prayer. That is not their aim. They are openings to a few themes that Saint Augustine held dear that we have chosen so that, led by him, we can, in his light, pray as he prayed. Saint Augustine always speaks to us in the deepest part of our heart. He inflames anyone who comes close to him.

1

Prepare to Welcome the Lord

Focus Point

God initiates a prayerful relationship with us by calling us to be with him in prayer. We decide whether to run from this call or to call on God's grace and turn to him in prayer. The depth of our prayer lives is dependent on how willing we are to open ourselves up to God in prayer. We can be totally open to him by his grace and if we are willing, allowing him to be a part of every aspect of our lives.

It is you who makes God either far or near. Love and he will come close. Love and he will dwell in you (Ser 21, 2).

Your prayer is a conversation with God" (En in ps 85,7). In order to have a conversation with someone, we must, first of all, feel that they are close to us. And often, we do not feel that way about God. When we speak to him, he seems absent, far away from us and our words just fall into a void.

However, Saint Augustine felt God close to him. He spoke to him just as a child speaks to his father: "And I chatter with you, my brightness, my wealth, and my salvation, Oh Lord, my God" (Conf IX, 1,1). And in the presence of God, Augustine meditated, questioned himself, and multiplied his questions. Everything spoke to him of God and he never stopped speaking to God. For him, God was not an abstract reality, but a person to whom we can truly speak. God has a heart that beats like our heart. Furthermore, God travels along life's roads with us. God's will and his desire is to be with us. That is why he liked to call himself "Emmanuel" (God-with-us). And Saint Augustine is truly very sensitive to this living and loving presence of God. He felt God close to him and close to us.

You are the life of souls, the Life of lives.
You are within me, more deeply than my
deepest soul (Conf III, 6,10).

However, Augustine had not always felt this
presence of God in his life. We must, therefore,
analyze his difficulties in prayer and the conditions that are favorable to pray to God or to
pray in a better way. Saint Augustine's difficulties in prayer are our own difficulties. We see
ourselves in him.

In order to pray, or better our prayers to
God, it is not enough just for God to speak to
us or to address us. It is absolutely necessary
that we be sensitive to his presence, that we feel
him close to us. Yet, quite often, we lack this
sensitivity; our eyes become blind to his presence and our ears become deaf to his voice. In
order to pray, we must, once again, then, find
this sensitivity that we are lacking. This sensitivity is a sensitivity of the heart.

It is not with our eyes, but with our heart
that we must seek God. But, just as, in
order to see our sun, we purify the eyes
of our body, by whose grace we can see
the light, it is the same if we want to see
God, let us purify the eyes which allow
us to see him (In Joh ep 7,10).

In order to feel God close to us, we must
then purify the eyes of our heart. The eyes of

our heart are quite often old, sick, and injured.
We are just like the disciples were after the
resurrection of Jesus. Jesus was there, next to
them, and the Gospel tells us: "Jesus himself
came and went with them, but their eyes were
kept from recognizing him" (Lk 24:15–16). To
recognize is to be born to the other; a sort of
identification with what we know. And it is
love that identifies us to another. We are what
we love in him.

In order to know God, to feel him close to
us, we must begin by loving him and, more-
over, become love ourselves, for God is Love.
To know God is to be born to the Love. Saint
John said it clearly: "Everyone who loves is
born of God and knows God. Whoever does
not love does not know God, for God is love"
(1 Jn 4:7–8).

However, in the first place, love is a gift.
To love is to become a gift. The gift offered
no longer belongs to us, it belongs to the one
to whom we offer it. God is Love and, by that
very fact, he gives himself and offers himself
entirely to us. God is like a ray of sunshine.
The ray never comes back on itself to contemplate itself. It simply seeks to shed light upon us
and fill us with light. And God gives himself to
us because he loves us. He is present for us in
all circumstances and all of life's events.

This presence of God in our lives is a living presence. And it is this presence that gives us assurance in our life. God makes us come into being. God encourages us to live. All things shine with his presence because they have come from him. In reality, it is not God who is in us, it is rather we who are in him. God holds and supports us in his hands.

My God, I would not exist, I would not exist at all unless you existed in me. Rather, I would not exist, if I didn't exist in you, from whom, through whom, and in whom everything exists (Conf I, 2,2).

Love is God's life. And because God loves us, we exist. To feel God next to us is to feel his creative love upon us: we feel loved by him. The biggest problem that we all face, at the moment of prayer, is to feel this love that God has for us, for us to feel loved by God.

However, to feel God's love, we must begin by purifying our heart, purifying our love.

Begin to love ... as the amount of love grows in you ... you begin to feel God (En in ps 49,5).

As much as we become love ourselves, we will experience God. To learn to pray, then, is to learn to love.

In order to live with God, in order to enter into communication with him, it is not enough just to reflect; we must, above all, know how to give of ourselves, how to offer ourselves. God gives himself to us, but in proportion to our gift of ourselves to him. It is the gift of ourselves that takes us towards God. But love doesn't reduce itself simply to make things happen for someone; it is a much deeper reality. To love someone is to enter into communion with that person, to rejoice in that person's presence, and to pass time in that person's company. In order to pray, then, we must enter into our own heart in order to seize it so we can give it. We pray just as we love; we pray just as we give of ourselves.

When we discover God's love for us, this love cures the insensitivity of our heart. We enter into prayer just as we enter into a friendship: by a path of trust and faith. Saint Augustine was very conscious of this and never stopped repeating it to us.

Saint Augustine, at the very beginning of his *Confessions*, clearly stated the problems of the conditions for prayer and praying effectively:

Grant me, Oh Lord, to know and understand whether I should first invoke you or praise you; whether I should first know you or invoke you. But, who invokes you without knowing you? For, he who does not know you might invoke another being instead of you. Or, are you invoked in order that you may be known? Indeed, "How are they to invoke him in whom they have not believed? Or how are they to believe, if no one preaches?" (see Rom 10:14). And they shall praise the Lord that seek him. For those who seek shall find him and those who find him shall praise him.

May I seek you, Oh Lord, by invoking you, and may I invoke you by believing in you: for you have been preached to us. My faith invokes you, Oh Lord, that faith which you have given to me, which you have breathed into me through the humanity of your Son, through the ministry of your preacher (Conf I, 1,1).

This text introduces us to the most profound dynamism of prayer. It also offers us the conditions that we must fulfill in order to pray.

At the beginning of prayer, there is always a call from God. We do not take the initiative to pray. It is God who calls us to pray.

We pray as we love. And we pray because God loved us first. Prayer, then, is a grace that God grants us: "This is love, not that we loved God but that he loved us … " (1 Jn 4:10). God never stops coming to us and he invites us to come to him. By everything that surrounds us, he never stops telling us: "Love me!"

This imperative expression, "Love me!" breaks our self-sufficiency and gives birth to an intimate relationship in us with him; it renders us able to love him. And it is this invitation to love him that constitutes the beginning of all true prayer. The initiative for prayer, then, comes from God himself.

Love the one who first felt love. And God shows us his love, above all, by Jesus, by the mystery of his Incarnation. Jesus is the true revelation of the love of the Father for us: "For God so loved the world that he gave his only Son ..." (Jn 3:16).

The first problem for us to be able to pray is to feel this love that God presents and welcome it into our heart. And the welcome of God's love into our life is faith. Faith is the happiness we have to feel that we are loved by God, to offer him our trust and allow ourselves to be guided by him.

> It is faith that prays, the faith that is given
> to the one who doesn't pray, that faith
> without which, he certainly couldn't pray
> (Ep 194,10).

And faith pushes us to bring us closer and closer to God, to give ourselves to him. Faith makes the desire to be with God spring forth from our heart. It is found at the source of love when it is lacking the satisfaction of a blessed life. And this desire to be with God, to unite ourselves with him, and to understand him is already a prayer in itself: "The desire to understand is a prayer to God" (Ser 152,1).

Furthermore, the duration of the desire is the same as the duration of the prayer. Yet the one who desires seeks the object of his desire. We seek what we desire. That is why there is no search for God if the desire to meet him is lacking. But the one who truly seeks God, always finds him in the end. God gives of himself to the one who gives of himself to him. Prayer, then, unites us to God, deifies us in a way. It introduces us into the very mystery of God.

> The Holy Trinity of God, the Father, the Son, and the Holy Spirit come to us while we come to them; they come into us by helping, we go in obedience; they come into us by illuminating, we go by looking; they come into us by fulfilling us, we go to them by welcoming them (In Joh ev 76,4).

And that is when the prayer of praise spurts forth from our heart to express our happiness for our meeting with him. Those who find God feel so happy that they can only manifest their happiness by a song of praise. Prayer introduces us, to a certain extent, into the vision of God.

There, we rest and will see; we will see and we will love; we will love and we will praise. That will be at the end, without end. And what other goal do we have, if not to reach the kingdom that has no end? (De civ Dei 22, 30, 5).

Reflection Questions

Do I feel God calling me to enter into prayer with him? How do I respond to this prayer? Do I embrace this call or do I run from it, fearing the new life that might accompany a prayerful relationship with the Divine? In what way(s) is God calling me to be with him? In meditation on Scripture, in the devotion of the rosary, in daily participation of the Mass? How much of myself am I willing to give over to God?

2

Come Back to Your Heart

Focus Point

The heart is our center. We must reflect deeply on the center of our person before we pray, so that we bring our true selves to God in prayer. We should not bring who we think we are, or what others tell us to be, or even what we think God wants us to be. Rather, we are to come to God simply as who we are in the present. God loves us for who we are, right here, right now. Knowing ourselves is the first step in coming to know God.

Come back to your heart, and from there, to God,
for the path is not long from your heart to God (Ser
311,13).

Christ is inside you, that is where he dwells. Present
him with your prayer (En in ps 141,2). 42

P rayer is an affair of the heart. God speaks
to us in our hearts and we must address
ourselves to God through our hearts. In order
to pray, we must, then, enter into our hearts.

The heart designates the center of ourselves.
It is the center where the personal operations
of knowledge, choice, freedom, and love have
their origins. We can then speak of the heart
of a person as we speak of the "heart" of a
problem. The heart is the deepest root of our
behaviors. But we often run the risk of living
our lives from the outside, starting from what
we say, in the fashion of the times. And, at that
particular moment, instead of living (actively),
we are lived (passively), we are only masking
ourselves. In order to meet God and enter into
communion with him, we must begin by being
ourselves. God is the Truth and in order to
enter into communion with him, we must be
true: "Those who do what is true come to the
light" (Jn 3:21). And to be true and to be ourselves is the first condition to be able to pray,

according to Saint Augustine. That is why he addresses God to tell him:

> For you have loved the truth, since "those who do what is true come to the light." I want to "do what is true" in my heart, before you in confession; and in my writing, before many witnesses (Conf X, 1,1).

And in one of his first books, The Soliloquies, he asked the Lord to help him to know him and himself.

> All that I ask in my prayer is to know God and the soul; that is what I want (Sol 1, 2,7).

> I shall know you, you who knows me, I shall know you as I am known! Virtue of my soul, go deep into it and make it fit for you, so that you may have it and possess it, without stain or wrinkle (Conf X, 1,1).

Sadly, we often hide from ourselves. And just like Adam sought to hide himself in the trees, we also seek to hide ourselves from God who is present in our heart. And Saint Augustine tells us:

> You, Lord, were right before me; but I had abandoned myself and I was unable to find myself, much less you! (Conf V, 2,2).

Certainly, within us, the voice of our heart endlessly cries out to us of God's presence. But we often don't pay attention; we turn a deaf ear to him, yet God never stops crying out to us: "Where are you?" God wants to eliminate our desire to flee from ourselves. Do we agree to not escape this question from God? As long as we escape from God and the voice in our heart, our life will simply become only a distraction, we will walk and go nowhere and at that time, it will be impossible to pray. The return to ourselves is the beginning of our return to God.

> You were within and I was outside and it was there that I was looking for you, and I threw myself, disgraced as I was, upon the grace of the things you have made. You were with me but I wasn't with you; these things kept me far away from you, things which would not have existed if they had not existed in you (Conf X, 27,38).

To enter into our heart is to take a step back, to become silent within and around ourselves. The voice of the Lord is always at the risk of being drowned out by the noises that seek to inhabit us. We must be vigilant to the signs that proclaim God's presence to us. The Lord tiptoes alongside us and is heard by the one who awaits him with an attentive ear in his heart.

Interior silence, then, is absolutely necessary for us in order to enter into the heart and there, in the heart, listen to God who is speaking to us. Furthermore, in order to speak to someone, we need silence in order to reflect on what we are going to say to them. Silence must permeate our words. It is in all true prayer. In order to pray we need to be silent in the most intimate parts of ourselves.

We must, then, come back to our heart in order to meet ourselves, ourselves and God. Saint Augustine never stopped inviting us to dwell in our heart.

> Come back to your heart, and from there, to God, for the path is not long from your heart to God. All of the difficulties that are troubling you come from what is outside of you, you who are the exile of your own heart. You let yourself be moved by what is outside of yourself and you lose yourself. You are within, they are outside; gold, silver, and all kinds of money, clothes, clients, the family, and the flocks, they are all outside (Ser 311,13).

But in order to meet God and pray, it is not enough just for us to take a step back, to enter into our heart, for that is a fruitless return to ourselves. When we enter into ourselves, we run the risk of making our intimacy, our heart, a permanent dwelling and, at that moment, our search for God will stop midway through. We would make our "self" become the goal of our search, or even the center of our life. And everything will revolve around us, our problems, our cares and our difficulties. However, our dwelling is not our heart, but God. The heart is only God's dwelling, not God himself.

Our heart brings us always back to God. God, who created us in his own image and likeness. The image, by its very nature, is oriented totally towards what it represents. The image never comes back on itself, it is always sent back to what it represents. It never draws attention to itself, but to what it reflects. Our heart, the image of God, always brings us back to him.

> You made us for you and our heart is without rest as long as it doesn't rest in you (Conf I, 1,1).

Our heart is, then, turned towards God. And Saint Augustine called this orientation towards God love, desire and the weight of the soul. Love, then, is the life of our heart. When love is extinguished, the heart dies and ceases its search for God, for "it is through love that we seek him" (De mor eccl Cath, 17,31).

We are, then, by our nature, oriented towards God. He made us for him, and, in the same way, we cannot stop on the road which leads us to God. To stop would be to refuse to love; to refuse to desire God.

The most serious danger in our prayer life is the death of desire, discouragement in the face of difficulties. At that time, we have no interest in prayer. That is the presence of death in our lives.

In the Gospels, the sick are the clearest expression of those who stop on the path that leads us to the Lord. And that is where the Lord comes to say to us: "Stand up and walk" (Mt 9:5). The Lord invites us to stand up and get back onto the path: "Stand up." He asks us to leave our heart in order to fix our gaze on him alone: "Go beyond yourself, beyond your heart" (De vera rel 39,73). He even comes to help us: "My grace is sufficient for you, for power is made perfect in weakness" (2 Cor 12:9). God invites us to live. God invites us to love. God is always the carrier of a message of life. Saint Augustine endlessly takes the path of interiority, the path of the heart, in order to feel God in the deepest part of himself, to let himself be guided and enlightened by him. He recounts his experience to us.

This is what I do frequently: it gives me joy to take refuge in this pleasure, as much as I can take a break from necessary duties. In all these things which I experience in seeking your counsel, I find no safe place for my soul except in you, where my scattered parts are gathered together and no portion of me may depart from you. Sometimes, you have introduced me to a very unusual inner experience, to an incredible sweetness, which, if it reaches perfection in me, will be beyond my present knowledge.

But it will not happen in this life, for I fall back among these lower things, pulled down by troubling weights and I am absorbed again in ordinary affairs. I am held fast and I weep a great deal, but I am held quite firmly. So great is the burden of routine! Here, I am able to exist, but I don't want to; I wish to be there, but I cannot be; with respect to both, I am unhappy (Conf X, 40,65).

Interiority, then, is the spiritual exercise by which we enter into a living relationship with God. But this process of contemplation is already a grace. We must always ask the Lord for it so that he will grant it; for it is this grace of interiority that introduces us into prayer.

Reflection Questions

Before I bring myself to God in prayer, I must know what I am bringing. How do I come to better know myself in my life? Do I have a spiritual director or a counselor who can help me to better understand who I am? Do I run from those parts of my personality that frighten me, that I do not want to deal with because of their hold on me or because I am embarrassed by them and might be "found out" by myself, God, or others?

3

Oh Beauty That Is So Old, Yet So New

////////////

Everything we see in creation speaks to us of God. All things, even those things we see time and again and pay little to no attention to, can be viewed as the unique and fresh elements of God's creation. If we contemplate any element of God's creation, we find out very soon that it directs us back to God since a part of his loving, creating hand is within that object.

////////////

My interrogation was my looking upon them, and their reply was their beauty (Conf X, 6,9).

*T*oday, we lack a sense of contemplation. We are so busy with work and success that we only see people and things in the light of their usefulness and efficiency. Our gaze has become an icy one, without joy and, under this gaze, neither persons nor things have any mystery any longer for us. Everything becomes an instrument, everything is reduced to the state of an inert object, available for our use, destined to be transformed and used. We have lost the sense of mystery. We even pass alongside other people without looking at each other, each of us absorbed by the interest of the moment. The eyes of our heart are truly sick. We are lacking a sense of graciousness and praise. We must then find out how to regain the sense of wonder: to welcome things with new, pure eyes, with the eyes of God. We must know how to look at everything with God's gaze. And Saint Augustine comes to help us; he discovered God in everything that is around us: things, persons, events. For him, everything in the world cries out God to us.

Everything speaks to us of God. Everything is a sign, the word of God. In fact, God created everything. But to have created them was not to have made them once and for all. Creation was and is a continuous action by God. God created us, but he is not far away from us; he remains close; he holds and supports us in his hands.

God alone is the creator of natures, he
who produces nothing in a way that has
not been produced by him; who has no
workers that he has not created; and if
he removes, from his works, the power
which I call "manufacturing," then they
would fall into nothingness and be as
they were before being made (De civ Dei
XII, 26).

That is why Saint Augustine prayed:

I would not exist, my God, I would
not exist at all, unless you were in me.
Or rather I would not exist, if I hadn't
existed in you, from whom everything
exists, by whom everything exists and in
whom everything exists (Conf I, 2,2).

Everything is, by its very existence, in a
relationship with God. Things never hold us
for long; when we know to listen to them, they
send us back to God. They are but signs of God
and the sign, the good sign, never holds one. It
always sends one back to what it reflects. Each
time we get closer to them, we hear their voices
telling us: go to God, don't stop here with us.

I interrogated the earth and it answered:
"It is not I." All the things that are in it
uttered the same confession. I asked the
sea, the depths, the creeping things living

amongst the animals, and they replied:
"We are not your God; look above us."
... And I said to all the things which surround the entryways to my flesh: "Tell
me about my God since you are not him;
tell me something about him." With a
loud voice, they cried out: "He made us."
My interrogation was my looking upon
them, and their reply was their beauty
(Conf X, 6,9).

God speaks to us through all of the events
of our life. God directs and governs everything
and everything becomes a call, an admonition
of God. And God calls us to go towards him,
for, in him alone, we truly encounter rest and
happiness.

All sensory experiences are a call that God
makes to us to return to him. The problem that
arises is to know how to decode and discern
the divine meaning of all of these events. And
the first condition that must be met in order to
have an experience of God through contemplation of the universe is silence, but it must be a
silence that opens us to life's events; a silence
that listens and pays attention. "My interrogation was my looking upon them" (Conf X, 6,9).

The insistence with which the Gospel
invites us to vigilance is truly remarkable.
Saint Mark was vigilant, in a way, in the tes-

tament of Jesus. In the first place, vigilance is
the attitude of the one who sits vigil, the attitude of the watchman. And the watchman sits
vigil precisely when the whole world rests. He
passes the majority of the night in the midst of
silence. And to keep watch is a particular way
of looking and listening. It is to discern, in the
apparent calm of the night, the noises or creaks
that tell us of the presence of someone. To be
vigilant, then, is to know how to figure out
the signs of a presence. Our attention orients
our gaze and makes us discover what is hidden under insignificant appearances. Hidden
under the innocence of the most simple human
relationships, just as in the most regular of the
daily events of our lives, is where the traces of
God are hidden and only the person who goes
beyond what is immediate will be able to discover them. To be a watchman is to know how
to discern, in the obscurity of life, the traces of
God's light.

But vigilance always necessitates an interior
availability: silence and withdrawal. By that
very fact, in the attention, there is an asceti-
cism of the eyes and ears which purifies us of
so many noises which it doesn't let us hear and
so many imaginings that it doesn't let us see.
Be careful, it is to learn to listen and to listen
is, for us, to open ourselves up to a person other
than ourselves; it is the attitude of a disciple,

of one who lets himself be taught by another person. To listen is to know to welcome.

God never stops coming to us, but God never imposes himself upon us. He gives himself to those who seek him, to those who pay attention to his presence. The problem with the meeting with God is never to be found in God himself. He never stops knocking at our door. Everything speaks to us about God. Everything tells us to love him and to return to him. The problem with our meeting with God is in our capacity to wait for him, to pay attention to him. God gives himself to us, but according to our capacity to pay attention to him. God is everywhere.

However, to welcome God's word in this reality that surrounds us is, first of all, for us to be in a state of marvel before his beauty. Saint Augustine asked himself:

> Do we love anything but that which is beautiful? What, then, is beauty? What is it that attracts us and attaches us to the things we love? (Conf X, 13,20).

It is the marvel and splendor of a thing or a behavior that catches our eye and grasps our attention. Before this manifestation of God, we feel seized by the spark of his light and grandeur. Before the splendor of God, we could do nothing more than cry out:

You are great Lord, and worthy of praise;
your power is great and your wisdom is
limitless (Conf I, 1,1).

But, at the same time, we recognize that
we are quite far from God; his glory dazzles
us and at times, shows us our limitations and
poverty.

To praise you is the wish of a man who is
only a part of your creation, a man who
carries upon himself the evidence of his
sins and the evidence that you resisted
the proud (Conf I, 1,1).

Moses, before God's revelation in the burning bush "hid his face, for he was afraid to look
at God" (Ex 3:6). Simon Peter, a witness to the
miraculous catch of fish, said to Jesus: "Go
away from me, Lord, for I am a sinful man!"
(Lk 5:8). The glory of God makes us discover
the impurity of our heart. The prophet Isaiah,
before the glory of God, said: "Woe is me! I am
lost, for I am a man of unclean lips ... yet my
eyes have seen the king, the Lord of hosts!" (Isa
6:5). At this experience of the glory and splendor of God, we must not be fearful and afraid
and it mustn't be a means of distancing us from
God. God is available to us in an admirable
way, even an adorable one. We feel fascinated
by him, by his beauty and his bounty. We feel

drawn by him: "O Lord, you have enticed me, and I was enticed; you have overpowered me, and you have prevailed" (Jer 20:7). And Saint Augustine tells us:

You struck down my feeble gaze by the strength of your rays on me, and I trembled with love and fear (Conf VII, 10,16).

What is it that shines in me and pierces my heart without wounding it? I am both full of terror and ardor; full of terror in as much as I do not resemble him; full of ardor in as much as I do resemble him (Conf XI, 9,11).

And that is what we transform in ourselves through praise. We can't keep to ourselves what we feel in the depth of our hearts and we become songs of praise. To praise and adore is to recognize that God is God and to let God express himself in us.

You see what he did; love the Author of these marvels! Attach yourself to the one who is essential! Love the Creator! Did he not create you in his image, you who have the happiness to love him? (Ser 68,5).

Reflection Questions

One method of prayer involves choosing an object of God's creation and contemplating that object for a period of time. If I attempt this in my own prayer life, I can ask the following questions: In what ways does this object direct me to God? In what ways has this object been used throughout history to draw God's people closer to their Creator? How does the structure, order, and/or make-up of this object teach me something about the Source who created it?

4

"Oh Eternal Truth, You Are My God"

Focus Point

////////////

We must be open to God, always available to him and open to his transforming love. Though God is always inviting us, gently, to closer union with him, this does not mean he loves less at one time than at another. By God's continuous, ever-giving love, we are transformed, knowing and loving ourselves and God — and becoming more aware of God's love for us — to a greater degree.

////////////

We can only enter into the Truth through charity (Cont Faust Manich, 32,18).

*E*verything speaks to us of God. Everything is a sign for us to go to God. But we can't approach God as we approach just anything. We must approach God as we approach a fire: by letting ourselves be burned. In order to know God, we must be born to him. Our attitude before God must be, first of all, an attitude of listening and availability. It is the same attitude that Mary had at the time of the Annunciation: "Here I am, the servant of the Lord; let it be with me according to your word" (Lk 1:38). In reality, we approach God by welcoming him into our heart for it is not we who are going to him, rather, it is God who is coming to us. And we welcome God into us by letting him transform us.

And God reveals himself, first of all, as a being of plenty, as the most total and absolute perfection; he is eternal, even immutability itself. God is, then, the Being. The Scriptures tell us that God is "I am who I am" (Ex 3:14).

Then God had already told Moses (when he asked his name) through the angel: "I am who I am." This is what you said to the children of Israel: "I am has sent me to you" (Ex 3:14). "I am" is the name of the one who can only make changes. In fact, everything that changes ceases to be what it was and begins to be what it wasn't. The true being, the pure being, the authentic being, only the One who doesn't change has it. The One who possesses the true being is the one to whom we say: "You change them ... and they pass away, but you are the same" (Ps 102:26). What does "I am who I am" mean if it doesn't mean that I am eternal? What does "I am who I am" mean if it doesn't mean that I can't change? Such a name, then, is his name for eternity (Ser 7,7).

Saint Augustine often felt God as being eternal, immutable, the one who is beyond everything. And before God, he feels struck with silence and adoration. God is so great and full of beauty and bounty that he can't find the words to describe him. Before God's glory, we can only remain on our knees in a silence of adoration. Words are not adequate to describe God.

All that you imagine is not God, all that you understand by reflection is not him; in fact, if it was him, he couldn't be understood by reflection (Ser 21,2).

There is then no correspondence between what God is and our words. Words are lacking to describe God. The only expression that is worthy of God is one of silence; not of a silence that says nothing, but a silence that is so rich that all words impoverish it. The experience of God does not give us the means to explain it. The light of God is too dazzling for our intelligence. For us, God becomes truly incomprehensible. Each time that he reveals himself, it is to show us that he is even greater and more mysterious than we have ever imagined before. God reveals the immense gap between him and us. He is the All-Everything. No word could possibly explain it. He is indescribable.

When Moses understood what he was told: "I am who I am"; "I am has sent me to you" (Ex 3:14), he thought that it was difficult for man to understand. He saw that it was far from man's spirit. (...) Moses cried to himself: "I said in my ecstasy." What did he say? "Everyone is a liar" (Ps 116:11). Then, in this way, Moses saw, but he didn't completely understand, not what he saw, but what was said to him; he was unable to grasp it; also, inflamed with the desire to see the One who is "I am," he said to God: "Show me your glory" (Ex 33:18). Moses was then very far from this excellence of the divine essence and this put him into a type of despair. But because he lived his fear, God saved him from his despair by telling him: because I said: "I am who I am" and "I am has sent me to you," you understood what comprises the Being, but you have lost hope to grasp it (Ser 7,7).

This text shows us Saint Augustine's experience with God. We are incapable of grasping God and even less of describing him. And he finds great difficulty in communicating his experience with God to us.

To me, however, my discourse almost always displeased me. I vividly want to do better; I can experience it interiorly before I can begin to develop it using words. But when I judge myself to be inferior to the one that I had in my mind, I find myself too sad to discover that my tongue is not adequate for my spirit. I want my listener to grasp all that I think and I feel that I can't explain myself in a way that is successful. The reason for this is that this intuitive conception floods my soul, like a quick flash, yet my discourse is slow and greatly different from it (De cat rud, 2,3).

God seeks us. He wants to be with us. And we could go through all of the Scriptures and there, only find evidence of God's desire to be with us. God is not someone without a face; he has a heart that beats like our heart. But God never imposes himself upon us. God always respects our freedom. It is he who created it and that wasn't so he could violate it. God never says "I want" but simply "if you want." He suggests and invites. God doesn't impose himself on us. That is his discretion. He doesn't show himself in the strength of a hurricane or in an earthquake, but in the passage of a light breeze (see 1 Kings 19:11–13). God is love and because he is love, he has an absolute sense of respect for us. To love someone is to live in a way so that we can recognize them for what they are and not for what I would like them to be. Love always makes the other more of himself. For Saint Augustine, God was nothing but Love.

Removed from love, God is incomprehensible. Love, then is the route of access to God. We can only know God through love. Saint Augustine never stopped telling us this.

> Learn to love your enemy.... In as much as love grows in you, shaping you and bringing you to a resemblance of God, it will extend to the enemies so that you will be like the One who made his sun rise, not only on the good but also on the evil.... As you progress in resemblance, you will progress in love and you will begin to feel God (En in ps 49,5).

Love will be, for Saint Augustine, the key that allows us to enter into the most intimate life of God, into all of his mysteries. The mysteries of God, the mystery of the Trinity, of the Incarnation, of the Revelation, and so many others, will be made incomprehensible without love. That is why love is the way we must seek God. Furthermore, to know love is to know God. The one who doesn't know the meaning of loving, listening, or welcoming will never meet the Lord. We are as close to God as those who suffer and need us. Charity and sharing make us know God. God comes to us when we go to others. "Everyone who loves is born of God and knows God. Whoever does not love does not know God, for God is love" (1 Jn 4:7–8).

Reflection Questions

Do I have difficulty understanding that God loves me just as much now as he ever will? Do I often feel that I have to earn points (by obeying the laws and statutes of my religion) to deserve God's love? Does this recognition of God's unending love for me lessen the pressure I feel in my relationship with him? Does my growing awareness of God's love for me transform me into a more spiritual person, a person more likely to love others with the same kind of mercy and unconditional love I have known from God?

5

"You Will See the Trinity if You See Charity"

Focus Point

///////////

God is love, and the Trinity is the perfect example of that love. Just as God loves the Son, but is separate from him, God loves us but lets us be who we are, separate beings capable of choosing to love God in the same way (if not to the same degree) as he loves us. Jesus taught us how to love the Father — in praise and thanksgiving — the way he did as the Son, with the gift of the Holy Spirit.

///////////

When we came to charity, called God by the Holy
Scriptures, the mystery clarified itself somewhat
with the Trinity of the lover, the loved, and the love.
But this inexplicable light dazzled our gaze (De
Trinit 15,6,10).

*T*he mystery of the Trinity is the most important mystery of the Christian faith. All of the other mysteries — the mystery of the Incarnation, the Revelation, and the Eucharist, or no matter which other one — are only explanations of this mystery of the Trinity. Saint Augustine well understood the special place that this mystery of God must hold in our lives. It is the center and the foundation of his meditation and theological reflection. And, to this mystery, he dedicated a very personal book: (Treatise) On the Trinity. The mystery of the Trinity nourished his spiritual life and he also wants it to do the same for us.

The mystery of the Trinity is, first, a mystery of God and, because of this, our attitude with respect to him must be an attitude of adoration. We must approach him as Moses did to the burning bush: by "removing the shoes" of our heart. "Come no closer! Remove the sandals from your feet, for the place on which you are standing is holy ground" (Ex 3:5). In order to approach this mystery of God, we must then purify our heart, for it is the pure of heart who will see God.

In order to contemplate the mystery of the Trinity, we must make a conversion in our heart. Egoism, and all sins are sins of egoism, does not let us know people as they truly are. It makes us see everything in the light of our personal tastes and our own interests. Then, in reality, the one who sees everything in the light of egoism, in the light of sin, sees no one, he simply sees himself; he listens to no one, he only listens to himself.

> It is a serious error to believe that we can know the truth when we live in a state of disorder…. The person who lives thus can't contemplate the pure, complete, and immutable truth, attach himself to it and fix upon it for all eternity. We must then, before purifying our spirit, first believe what we can't understand; for the prophet righteously said: "If you don't believe, you don't understand" (De agone Christ, 13, 14).

Our attitude, in the face of the Trinity, must, then, be to purify our love, for only through love are we permitted to know God. Our knowledge of God is in proportion to our love.

> I see charity and, as much as I can, I fix the gaze of my spirit on it. I believe in the

Scriptures which say that God is charity and that the one who dwells in charity, dwells in God. But, when I see it, I don't see the Trinity there. But yes! You see the Trinity if you see charity (De Trinit 8,8,12).

And Saint Augustine got closer to the mystery of the Trinity also in an ambiance of prayer and humility. He was very conscious of the fact that God was too great for us to grasp.

Who understands the almighty Trinity? And who doesn't speak of it — if it really is of it we speak? It is a rare soul that knows of what it speaks when speaking of it. We discuss and argue, yet no one can see this vision in peace … (Conf XIII, 11,12).

God reveals himself to us through the mystery of the Trinity, that is to say, through the mystery of communion between the three divine persons. In this mystery, the Father bounteously gives of himself to the Son, and the Son to the Father, and this communion is made through the love of the Holy Spirit. The three persons are different, but never separated from one another; they are always in a union, in an intimate communion with each other. They make up the one unique God. The communion between the Father, Son, and Holy Spirit is so complete and profound that it is one unity. Yes, we believe that there is one God, but this God exists as a Trinity.

For Saint Augustine, the most profound reality of God was this communion between the divine persons. He never thought of a solitary God, but of the communion of the three divine persons. And this communion is the most perfect realization of charity.

God is charity because the Father, Son, and Holy Spirit are one (In Joh ep 10,5).

In effect, the one who God sent said God's words. He, himself, was the veridical God, and it was God who sent him: God sent God. Reunite these two, they are one God, the veridical God sent by God. Ask each of them, he is God. Not that each will be God and that they will be two gods, but each in particular is God and the two together are God. The charity of the Holy Spirit which unites them is so great, in fact, the peace of the unity is so perfect that when we ask about each, he replies that he is God and when asked about the Trinity, they reply that it is God.... Understand it this way: there are as many souls as there are humans; if they love each other, they will form a single soul; nevertheless, we can still speak of many souls when we speak of mankind, for their union will never reach this degree of perfection. Yet, to the contrary, you can say that there is one God, but you can't say that there are two or three gods. That underlines the supereminence and supreme perfection of this charity which can't be any greater (In Joh ev 14,9).

The most intimate part of God is Love. And the mystery of the Trinity is the most perfect fulfillment of what it means to love, of what it means to say that God is Love. Love helps us enter into the mystery of the Trinity.

By reflecting upon charity, which is called God in the Holy Scriptures (see 1 Jn 4:16), I began to understand, a little, the analogy of the Trinity being the lover, the loved, and the love (De Trinit 15,3,5).

The Holy Scriptures never speak about a God for himself, but about a God for us and with us. God, the Father, will be a phantom for us, a figment of our imagination if we don't see him as the Father of Jesus, as the Father who forgives us and who seeks us with an unending love, as a Father who has chosen us to become his children. The Father loves the

Son and, in his Son, he loves us all with all of
his heart. However, to love is to want the other
person for himself. And for the Son, so that we
become ourselves, the Father steps back and
removes himself. To love is to want the other
to exist. God the Father always remains very
discreet with respect to us. He loves silence. It
is the effect of his love for us. In reality there is
never love without poverty and humility. God
is silent to let us speak. God removes himself
but does so that we can be ourselves. And yet
the Father is never far away from us. He is
always at our side, but with a presence that is
full of discretion and respect. He doesn't show
himself unless he must in order to invite us to
him. To understand that God is our Father is
to enter into the most profound reality of love.
And, because we are very conscious that God
is our Father and that, to call him Father is to
call him a gift, in our prayers we always begin
by addressing ourselves to him by calling him
Father and by recognizing ourselves as being
his children through his only Son, Jesus Christ.

Our Father. This name evokes love; is
there anything more precious to children
than their father? And there is affection
in our prayers, since we say "Our Father";
and a certain hope to obtain what we
are asking for, since, even before asking for it, God already grants us a great

favor, the permission to call him "Our Father." What can he refuse his children in prayer, when he has already allowed them to be his children? (De ser Dmi in monte, 4,16).

And it is the same for the Son. He has no meaning for us if we don't see him as the one who was born in Bethlehem, lived in Nazareth, proclaimed the Good News, died on the cross, was arisen from the dead, and makes us God's children in his image. As children, we should welcome God and listen to him. Jesus, all throughout the Gospel, revealed himself as the Son of the Father. And his first attitude with respect to the Father was one of listening. He welcomed the will of the Father all the way to letting it dwell within him, letting it be one with him.

Everything in the Son carries the characteristic of "to be received." The Son is "to be received." He is a "loved being." And Jesus, all throughout the Gospel, revealed himself to us as the Son of the Father. He always refused to take credit for his mission, his works and his teachings, he said: "I have not come on my own" (Jn 7:28), and "I have not spoken on my own, but the Father who sent me has himself given me a commandment about what to say and what to speak" (Jn 12:49); and "I can do nothing on my own" (Jn 5:30). Jesus saw himself as the Son of the Father and he lived in a permanent state of thanksgiving. To give thanks and to give recognition of it is the clearest expression of the love of a son. And Jesus' prayer is, in the first place, a prayer of thanksgiving: "Father, I thank you for having heard me" (Jn 11:41); and "I thank you, Father, Lord of heaven and earth" (Lk 10:21). And Jesus taught us to give thanks, to become a son like he is the Son. And it is in recognition that we identify with him.

And it is the same for the Holy Spirit. He is the one who manifests the love of the Father and the Son at Pentecost for us, and it is he who opens the Scriptures to us, who makes us discover the life of God in them, and it is also he who made the unity of the Church. However, the Holy Spirit reveals himself to us as Love. The Holy Spirit is the gift of the Father to the Son and the Son to the Father.

> This Holy Spirit, according to the Holy Scriptures, is neither the Spirit of the Father, nor only the Spirit of the Son, but the two: in the same way, he teaches us this common charity of the Father and Son, through which they love each other mutually (De Trinit 15, 17,27).

And when he dwells in us, he makes us in his image; he makes us a gift to God and others; he makes us into prayer and communion. The action of the Holy Spirit manifests itself in us just as he manifested himself to the apostles at the time of the Pentecost, through a union with us all. It is the Holy Spirit that created the Church. Our love is the effect of the presence of the Holy Spirit in our hearts. The mystery of the Trinity is not an abstract mystery which has nothing to do with our daily life. It is a living mystery: the mystery of God's life and our own life. Separated from this mystery, our life is incomprehensible. The mystery of the Trinity reveals the most profound being of God and our truth to us: what we are, and what we must be.

Reflection Questions

Do I model my relationship with God after the relationship I see between Jesus the Son and God the Father in Scripture? Do I meditate on the mystery of the Trinity during my prayer life? How might a deepening awareness of the perfect love that is shared in the Trinity help me to nurture and support the relationships in my life?

6

The Bounty and Goal of the Scriptures Is Love

Focus Point

//////////////

We will always find Christ in the Scriptures. If we do not find him there, then we have misunderstood the Scriptures. Both the Scriptures and Jesus Christ are the "Word of God" — one put onto paper, one made flesh. The meaning is the same in both: to "illuminate the heart that we might see the truth." Each "Word" points us toward that love for which we should strive.

//////////////

*My strengths, oh brothers, are such small things, but
the power of the word of God is great: may they be
as great in your heart (Ser 42,1).*

*F*or Saint Augustine, the Holy Scripture is
the word of God; it is the "Word-made
flesh of God" and by that very fact, the second
person of the Holy Trinity. To get close to the
Holy Scripture is to get close to the Son in the
mystery of the Trinity. It is, then, at the interior
of the Trinity that we must read and meditate
on the Scriptures.

The Word-made-flesh of God, through the
mystery of the Incarnation, became human; he
came to us to reveal God's life to us and, at the
same time, to offer us a means to share in it.

The Scriptures are, in a certain measure, a
sort of Incarnation of the Word-made-flesh of
God. In it, the Word creates itself just like our
language so that it can be understood by us and
indicates the path that leads us to the Father.
Reading and meditating on the Scriptures
opens us to a certain "vision of God."

> The Word of God is one and it spreads
> itself by the Scriptures. It is proclaimed
> by a whole multitude of saints, yet it
> remains the single unique word. This
> word, being God at the beginning,
> according to God, and by that very fact,

has no syllables, for in it, there is no time.
And we shouldn't be surprised, if, by reason of our infirmity, it descended all the
way to making it our words when it took
on the weakness of our body (En in ps
103, 4,1).

Saint Augustine said, on numerous occasions, that "the Word-made-flesh made itself
our words," and he always put the Scriptures in
relationship to the mystery of the Incarnation.
Both are only expressions of the humility of
God and we must never separate them. Christ,
then, is the light that allows us to understand
the mystery of the Scriptures.

We should bring everything to Christ
if we want to walk on the right path of
intelligence.... If, in a particular passage of Scripture, we can't understand
the meaning, let us not separate it from
Christ ... as long as we have not come
to find Christ, we have not truly understood the text (En in ps 96,2).

The Holy Scriptures are, in a certain way,
the "incarnation of the Word-made-flesh" and
its goal is the same as the Incarnation: to illuminate our heart so that we can see the truth.
The Scriptures are a means of aid that the Lord
grants us in order to more easily go to him.

The Scriptures, for us, are, at the same time, both "examples" and "sacraments." Saint Augustine never stopped telling us that the Scriptures were, above all, the mirror in which we must contemplate ourselves. They reveal not only who we are to ourselves, but also, and above all, what we should be. We must, then, know how to make our lives conform to them. The Scriptures are not books of knowledge about the things of the world which don't touch anything in our lives; they are books of life, books of our lives, and we must know to recognize ourselves in them.

> It is a mirror that is proposed to you in this text; see if you are what it proclaims; if you are not yet, moan so that you will be. The mirror will make you recognize your face; in the same way, it can't flatter you, don't flatter yourself. Its bright purity shows you what you are and, if you are displeased with yourself, seek to no longer be that way (En in ps 103, 1,4).

But the Scriptures are not all simply "examples" and "mirrors," they are also "sacraments" for us. They transform the one who meditates on them. The meditation on the Scriptures introduces us into the mystery of God. The one who welcomes the word of God is changed and transformed by it. In the same way, in the

Eucharist, by welcoming the word of God, the bread and the wine on the altar become the body and the blood of Christ. A transformation like that is made in the one who listens to and lets himself be guided by the Scriptures.

Saint Augustine approached the Scriptures as we approach the Eucharist. Both constitute, for him, the bread of the spirit, the bread that supports and solidifies faith, hope, and charity. He devoted himself, daily, to his study and meditation and, at times, he didn't stop breaking the bread of the Scriptures through his commentaries by helping us to better understand them.

The meditation of the word of God must be the foundation of our life. But this meditation must be much more than an intellectual exercise. It is a means of communication, a dialogue with God. The Scriptures are the words that God addresses to us even today and in the concrete situation we are in currently. We must know how to welcome them, how to let ourselves be shaped by them. Saint Augustine asks us to read the Scriptures in a living way. By seeking, surely, what it signifies, but above all seeking the personal message that God is addressing to us.

In the meantime, in order to approach the Scriptures in a good way, we need to prepare ourselves. We don't read the Scriptures as just any other book. They are the word of God and we must approach them as we approach the Word-made-flesh of God.

From the Holy Scriptures, the Word-made flesh of God created our language, he took the body of our speech. In order to enter into a meditation of the word of God, we need an attitude of humility. God doesn't have great discussions with us. He speaks to us like his children and it is like children that we must become in order to understand.

> To rid the human spirit of all of its errors, the Holy Scriptures, which puts itself at the disposal of the little ones, neglected no category of thing to which the language was able, if we could say, to nourish our spirit, in order to allow it to grow, little by little, in a way, all the way to the divine and sublime realities (De Trinit 1,1,2).

Humility puts us in an attitude of welcome and listening. It reveals the infinite breech that separates us from God, but, at the same time, it puts us in an atmosphere of amazement before the manifestation of the glory of God. Humility awakens the capacity to be marvelled within us and makes us discover God. We must do it ourselves in such a way so that the marvel brings us to the point of being able to feel the glory of God. And it is humility that gives us the eyes and ears to see and hear God. It makes us sensitive to the Word.

> If you elevate yourself, God distances himself from you; if you humble yourself, he leans towards you (Ser 21,2).

In order to enter into the mystery of the Scriptures, we also need prayer. More than that, we need to address the Word of God just as we enter into prayer. Prayer is a dialogue with the Lord. In it, God speaks to us and we speak to God.

> Your prayer is a conversation with God. When you read, it is God who is speaking; when you pray, it is with God that you are speaking (En in ps 85,7).

The Word of God is not abstract or impersonal. It is what God addresses to us here and now. To welcome it, we must begin by being silent within ourselves and having silence surround us. Before listening to the Word, we must learn to listen to its silence.

> From the disturbances which are outside, the Scriptures call us back then, to the inside; from what is happening on the surface to the eyes of man, it calls us to the inside. Consult your conscience, question it. Don't look at what is flower-

ing on the surface, but the root that is in
the ground.... Go back into yourselves,
brothers; and in everything you do, see
that you have God as a witness (In Joh
ev 8,9).

To understand the Scriptures, we must
know how to recognize the light of charity.
Charity is the criteria for discernment in order
to interpret it well. Saint Paul tells us: "Love
is the fulfilling of the law" (Rom 13:10); Saint
John said: "God is love" (1 Jn 4:8). Scripture,
then, is the Word of Love. Through it, we can
discover what Love is.

The major point of all that we have said
... is to understand that the bounty and
the goal of the Law, like all of the divine
Scriptures, is love.... No matter who
imagines to have intellectually understood the Scriptures or at least a part of
them without edifying this double love
of God and neighbor, they have yet to
understand them (De doct Christ 1, 35,
39; 36, 40).

To understand the mystery of the Scriptures,
we must also invoke the Holy Spirit. It is he
who inspired them and it is he, alone, who
makes them understandable to us: "When the
Spirit of truth comes, he will guide you into

all the truth" (Jn 16:13). In the same way as he descended upon the Blessed Virgin Mary and, in her, the Word was made flesh, he must also descend upon us so that the Word is made the flesh of our flesh. When we meditate on the Scriptures, we must relive the Pentecost. We must pray, invoke the Holy Spirit and know how to wait, just like Mary and the disciples did.

The principle that guides Saint Augustine in his way of reading, meditating on, and interpreting Scripture is that it is, in the first place, the work of the Holy Spirit, the place where he is present and active. We must, then, read it in the same spirit in which it was written.

Reflection Questions

Do I incorporate reading the Bible into my prayer life? In what ways? Do I see the Incarnational relationship between the Scriptures (the "Word of God") and Jesus (the "Word-made-flesh")? How does each lead me to a deeper relationship with the Divine? Would other methods of scriptural prayer (lectio divina, for example) benefit my prayer life? Do I recognize the role of the Holy Spirit in the formation of sacred Scripture? How does this affect the way I read the Bible?

7

Christ Was Born So We Can Be Reborn

Focus Point

////////////

The eye of the heart must be healed, and all impurities within it cleaned out, if we are to see God. As God humbled himself by becoming flesh in the Incarnation, we must humble ourselves, making ourselves available to God, by stripping away the distractions that obstruct us from loving him. In the Incarnation, Jesus Christ shared in the experience of being human, uniting the human and the Divine, so that we might return to God.

////////////

Yes Christ was born: may no person ever doubt that
he can be reborn (Ser 189,3).

We must know how to recover the sensitivity of our heart in order to feel God close to us and listen to him. But it is God himself who helps us achieve this purification of heart.

> Our total job in this world is to heal this eye of our heart which makes us see God. It is to this end that the celebration of the holy mysteries is ordered, to this end that the Word of God is preached, towards this end that the moral exhortations of the Church, which aim at correcting social morals, are directed ... it is in this sense, finally, that all of the actions of the divine and holy writings are practiced, by healing the interior eye of all impurities that conceal it from the sight of God (Ser 88,5).

It is certain that everything speaks to us of God, that everything is an invitation from God to love him. But, the place where these words speak with the most strength and clarity is in the mystery of the Incarnation. In this mystery, God, himself, comes to us, he knocks at our door to awaken us to his presence.

The mystery of the Incarnation was also the mystery of Saint Augustine's conversion and it must also be the mystery of our own conversion. Up until the moment when Augustine discovered this mystery, God had been a far-off being for him who dwelled outside and beyond everything. And that is when God humbled himself, made himself small, just like us. Augustine felt seized by God's humility and even more so since, in his opinion, humility is an expression of love. Humility is availability, listening, and putting oneself at the service of another. That is why the one who loves is truly humble:

> The Son of God, who is Truth himself, put truth within our reach by becoming a man (De civ Dei XI, 2).

But if God came to us, it was to bring us to him; he makes himself our path, the milk to feed the children that we are. God, through the mystery of the Incarnation, reveals, to us, the path that leads us to him.

> I sought the way to attain the strength that would make me able to enjoy you. And I didn't find it until I embraced the Mediator between God and man, Jesus Christ, as a man who is above all things. God blessed forever. He calls out and says: "I am the way, the truth and

the life"; who combined the food (which
I was too weak to take) with the flesh,
since the Word was made flesh, so that,
your Wisdom, by which you have created all things, becomes the milk for our
infancy (Conf VII, 18,24).

The mystery of the Incarnation is the mystery to which Augustine came back throughout
his entire life; it is the mystery which reveals
the true reality of God to us.

The Incarnation of Christ manifests, on
the part of God, his willingness to share in
our own existence in order to help us return
to him. Through his Incarnation, God bows
down towards us and offers his hand to help
us up. This initiative of love, alone, on the part
of God, permits him to explain how his Only
Son, the Word of God became flesh.

In truth, we can only go to God by following the path that God, himself, took to come
to us.

If you seek the Truth, follow the path; for
the path is also the Truth. This is where
you must go, the route you must take....
It is through Christ that you will come to
Christ. How can you go to Christ through
Christ? To Christ the God through Christ
the man. Through the Word made flesh

to the Word who was next to God at the beginning (In Joh ev 13,4).

The mystery of the Incarnation manifests the gift that God gives us; it was he who gave himself to us. He wants to make us his children, in the image of Jesus, his only Son. God was born so that we could be reborn to him. The birth of Jesus is a call to be reborn to God.

In the mystery of the Incarnation, Jesus is given to us so that the face of God illuminates our own face. But the birth of Jesus at Christmas is much more than a historical event. It is, above all, the presence of God amongst us; even more than that, it offers us all of the conditions which we need to be able to recognize God in our lives. God wants to be born, God wants to dwell in our lives, and the conditions for Jesus' birth are the same as those for the birth of God in our hearts. That is why it is of utmost interest to know the circumstances that surround Jesus' birth: they continue to fulfill themselves in our lives.

Yes, Truth was born on earth because Christ was born of the Virgin. And justice looked upon us from heaven so that, through it, mankind would regain wisdom, those who, through injustice, had fallen into foolishness. We are mortal; sin destroys us; we carry the burden of our punishment. All mankind, by being born, begins life by being unhappy. It is useless to consult a prophet about this point. Ask the one who was born! Look at his tears! And when such a person on earth was under the curse of God, what blessing then appeared suddenly? "The Truth was born on earth." He created everything, and he is amidst everything! The one who created the day, saw the day. Christ, the eternal Lord who has no beginning with respect to the Father, now has the celebration of his birth. And if he hadn't had a human birth, he, the Word of God, from the beginning, we couldn't have obtained the new birth of grace. He was born so that we could be reborn. Yes, Christ was born; may no one doubt that they can be reborn (Ser 189,3).

Jesus was born, first of all, in the middle of the night. The night has a sense of darkness and, by that very fact, of disorientation. In the middle of the night, we feel lost, we no longer know where we are walking. The night is an expression representing sin. Dangerous things happen during the night and we are fearful. We aren't sure of ourselves. And, at that moment, in the middle of the night, we run the risk of stopping ourselves for we fear getting involved.

We seek a place of refuge, a grotto, whether it is in our past or in our ideas, in order to justify our behavior, we begin to dream.

That is the meaning of the night. And it is in the middle of the night, in the midst of this obscurity, that Jesus was born. And Christ is the light in the middle of the night through his humility; as much as pride obscures our heart, humility lightens it up.

Christ was born in the middle of our night to illuminate us: "I am the light of the world. Whoever follows me will never walk in darkness" (Jn 8:12). And it is for each of us to know how to orient his own life according to the light of Jesus, following his star. Jesus in Bethlehem offers us a new birth.

At the beginning there was the Word and the Word was in God; everything had been made by him; and here the Word was made flesh and he dwells amidst us. Listen how this was done. Assuredly to the eyes of those who believe in his name, he gave the strength to become children of God; and those to whom he had given the power to become children of God must never think that it is impossible to become children of God. The Word was made flesh and he dwells amidst us. Don't think that it is too much for you to become a child of God: for you, the one

who was the Son of God became the son
of mankind. If he had made himself anything less, he who was the most, could
he have not made us less than we are, we
could have been something greater? He
descended to us and we wouldn't rise up
to him? (Ser 119,5).

The second characteristic that surrounds
the birth of Jesus is solitude. Saint Luke tells
us: "While they were there, the time came for
her to deliver her child. And she gave birth to
her firstborn son and wrapped him in bands of
cloth, and laid him in a manger, because there
was no place for them in the inn" (Lk 2:6–7).

The most radical and profound truth of this
is that, there, where they had enough space for
everyone else, they had no place for Jesus. And
Jesus was born alone outside of the town, just
as he died on the cross, alone, outside of the
walls of Jerusalem.

We are always infected by a possessive
"me": we want to be unique; the only one in
the world, leaving no place for anyone else.
We live enclosed upon ourselves. As much as
the life of God unites, for it is communion and
communication, sin, all sin, distances us from
each other. And, from that time on, we live in
a world without sharing, a world that is closed
upon itself where the reign of solitude is the

most total. And it is precisely into this world without sharing and communion that Christ was born. Christ came to unite us, to reunite us around him, for true communion is made in him; it is "to have only one heart and one soul in God" (Reg 1,1).

It is not a true friendship unless you cement it between those who are united to you through the charity that is spread in our hearts by the Holy Spirit who has been given to us (Conf IV, 7,7).

The shepherds came to Jesus as did the Magi. He reunited around himself all persons and all peoples.

Let us cry out in a loud voice: "Glory to God in the highest, and peace on earth to men of good will." Let us study, with all the strength of our attention, the meaning of these divine words, these divine praises, this angelic song; meditate on it with faith, hope, and charity. For, conforming to what we believe, to what we hope, and to what we desire, we also glorify God in the highest, when, at the resurrection of our body, which will have become spiritual, we will be transported to the heavens, before Christ; as long as, during our stay on earth, we have united peace and good will (Ser 193,1).

Jesus, by his birth, deemed to become the companion of our solitudes. The star of Jesus shines in the midst of the darkness in order to make us see the others and open us to communion. That is why, after Jesus's birth, the angels of heaven communed with us; the shepherds took to the roads to seek Jesus, and furthermore, they sought to tell others the good news: "When they saw this, they made known what they had been told them about this child; and all who heard it were amazed at what the shepherds told them" (Lk 2:17–18). They became the first missionaries of Jesus. They fulfilled the song of the angels: "Glory to God in the highest heaven, and on earth peace among those whom he favors" (Lk 2:14).

Reflection Questions

In what ways do I seek to "purify the eye of my heart"? Do I practice self-denial in some way? Do I practice self-discipline in the structure of my prayer life? In what other ways do I humble myself, making myself available to God and readying myself to listen to him in prayer? Do I praise God for and meditate on the Incarnation during my praying?

8

"Here Is the Newborn Christ; Let Us Grow With Him"

Focus Point

We must make room in our hearts, in our lives, so that Jesus can be born into us. Love is important to knowing God because loving moves us beyond our selves, beyond our selfishness, and allows the love of Christ to work through us. We then become more of a participant of the love that grows between God and ourselves and the people we encounter. We must welcome the newness of each day, of every person and situation, and, working as an instrument of God, we must seek

95

to bring God's love to everything we encounter. By this, we will grow with the Christ inside of us.

////////////

You lift yourself up better if it is the one who never falls who helps you up. The one who never falls came down to you; you had fallen, he descended, he offered you his hand; you couldn't get up on your own: seize the hand of the one who descended to you so that you will be lifted up by the one who is strong (En in ps 95, 7).

The mystery of Christmas is our own mystery. Christ's birth must be our own birth to God. Through his birth, Jesus teaches us to be born, for we are called to become children of God and to call God "Our Father."

However, the conditions for Jesus' birth are the same for our own birth to God. On numerous occasions, the Gospels speak to us about the Kingdom of God: of its creation, how it grew, and how we could gain entry into it. The Kingdom of God is rightly this small child of Bethlehem who wants to grow in our lives, who wants to be born into our hearts. We must then know how to meet Jesus, welcome him, and grow with him. And the conditions that exist in order to meet and welcome him are offered to us by the mystery of Christmas.

It is very interesting to analyze the different behaviors of the people who existed in the midst of this mystery of Christmas: their behaviors are our own behaviors — those that draw us closer to and distance us from Jesus.

The Residents of Bethlehem

Speaking about the birth of Jesus, Saint Luke tells us: "While they were there, the time came for her to give birth to her child. And she gave birth to her firstborn son and wrapped him in bands of cloth, and laid him in a manger, because there was no place for them in the inn" (Lk 2:6–7).

The harshest truth of this event is that there, where there was a place for everyone, there was no place for Jesus. The residents of Bethlehem were so occupied by their work, their cares, their occupations and preoccupations that there — where there was space for everyone — there was no place for the Lord, and he was born elsewhere.

This passage from the Gospels is perhaps self-fulfilling in our lives. We are so taken by our occupations and preoccupations that, in our hearts, there, where there is a place for everyone, there is no place for the Lord. And today, just as back then, he has to be born elsewhere, far from us and far from our hearts. So that Jesus can be born into our lives, we must make a place for him in our hearts.

Furthermore, so that Jesus comes to be born into our lives, we must, above all, know to await him. Jesus is a gift, but the gift is only received by the one who awaits it. However, if we have no need for him, if we expect nothing of him, we will let him pass us by. The mystery of Christmas puts our life into question. Do we truly await Jesus? Do we truly feel the need for Jesus? To await Jesus is to offer him our heart. But to offer him our hearts, we must first possess it. By closing the doors of their homes, the residents of Bethlehem closed the doors of their hearts and their love and never recognized Jesus. The light didn't enter into them and they became darkness.

Here, down on earth, fraternal charity, then, is the path to know God; God is known through this experience of love. That is why Saint Augustine said: "We only enter into Truth through charity" (Cont Faust Manich, 32,18).

The residents of Bethlehem were rich. Their hearts were filled with material things. They thought only of themselves and of their reputations before their families and friends. And a person who is preoccupied by material things or by himself closes himself to others and does not recognize the Lord.

God is God because he gives of himself. He is infinite love, infinite gift and, by that very fact, he has nothing for himself. God is a poor person and only a poor person can know what poverty is. Those who are rich and full of vanity don't know God. They lack the sensitivity of heart.

The Shepherds

Faced with the behavior of the residents of Bethlehem, Saint Luke proposes the behavior of the shepherds to us as a subject for reflection: "In that region there were shepherds living in the fields, keeping watch over their flock by night. Then an angel of the Lord stood before them, and the glory of the Lord shone around them, and they were terrified" (Lk 2:8–9).

In Israel, the shepherds were not seen in a good light, for they usually lived on the fringe of the Jewish community. They were children, poor people, and the downtrodden. And then the Lord came to them and knocked at their door! And they welcomed the Lord's call and met him. Today, like back then, it is simply the one who pays attention to others, who awaits something from others — the poor, the indigent, the one who is not enclosed by all types of walls — who will meet the Lord. In order to hear the footsteps of the Lord as he passes, we must be quiet. The Lord gives himself to the one who seeks him, to the one who awaits him.

The shepherds were poor and poverty in spirit is the condition that is absolutely necessary in order to have the experience of Jesus. Jesus, himself, told us: "... the poor have good news brought to them" (Mt 11:5). Those who are poor in spirit are those who don't look at themselves because their treasure is elsewhere. They are completely open to the light and to others.

> Humbly, I came; to teach you humility, I came; as a master of humility, I came. Whoever comes to me becomes humble, whoever joins me will be humble, for they will not do their own will, but God's (In Joh ev 25,16).

The path that leads to Jesus, the path that puts us on track to Jesus, is always poverty of heart. As in Bethlehem, it is in the poorest place in our lives, in the humblest corner, into the area that is the most abandoned, that Jesus continues to be born.

In order to meet Jesus, we must also know when to leave our lambs, the "flock" of our own ideas, our stubbornness, and our private desires and, like those who are truly poor, leave, just like the shepherds did. Like them, we will find Jesus.

King Herod

With King Herod and the Magi, we will find a behavior that is similar to both that of the residents of Bethlehem and the shepherds.

King Herod, like the residents of Bethlehem, led his life in reliance upon his power and authority. He listened to no one, for he needed no one. He only listened to himself. Because of this fact, he didn't hear the footsteps of Jesus as he passed, just as he didn't see the star of God. The ramparts that his egoism and vanity erected around his heart were higher than the ramparts which surrounded his castle. That is why he didn't make the least of moves to meet Jesus. He needed no one, he didn't need Jesus: he trusted no one. He believed only in his power and his knowledge.

It is in our interest to stop here and consider Herod's behavior. He was a pagan who had usurped the throne of Israel. He presumed to recuperate the prophesies to make others believe that they spoke of him and, even worse than that, he lied to the Magi. He had killed truth, innocence, and purity of heart, as much by hypocrisy and lies as by the massacre of the children and what they represented to God. "… unless you change and become like children, you will never enter the kingdom of heaven" (Mt 18:3).

Herod remained blind to the star of God, for he had killed the pure and innocent glance of the children. A heart that is righteous, pure, and honest is a condition that is absolutely necessary in order to meet God.

Faced with this attitude by King Herod, the Gospels propose the behavior of the Magi as a subject for reflection. They knew the movements of the stars and the revolutions of the planets. They knew the laws of nature. They were the wise men. And there they came to discover a star, in their sky, that didn't fit with their knowledge. They looked at this star more closely. They checked it. They questioned themselves. They opened themselves to it. Never did they say: "This is not possible." They sought and put themselves on the path to ask for counsel. Never did they close themselves upon themselves. The Magi had the souls of children. In order to meet the Child Jesus, we must conform to him. We must become children in order to have access to God. "... unless you change and become like children, you will never enter the kingdom of heaven" (Mt 18:3).

And still the Lord wants to heal us. In order to heal us, he became one of us. He was born amongst us in order to teach us to be born to ourselves. However, this birth requires us to change our lives and our regular way of living. We must become like children.

This conversion that we all must make is exactly this passage from the behaviors of the residents of Bethlehem to the shepherds, King Herod to the Magi and from vanity to humility. We must, then, know how to find our childhood again and we will get to it, on the condition that we want to open our eyes in order to see everything as God sees it.

Everything that we do here on earth, all our good works, our efforts, our praise-worthy ardors, and our innocent desires come to fruition as long as we seek nothing other than the vision of God. In fact, what could one seek if he already possesses God, and how could one satisfy someone to whom God isn't enough? What we want, what we seek, what we ardently desire is to see God. Who experiences this desire? Listen to these words: blessed are those who are pure of heart, for they will see God. Prepare, then, the eyes that should see him; for in order to use a comparison that is borrowed from exterior things, why do you want to see the rising of the sun with sick eyes? May your eyes be healthy, and you will contemplate this light with happiness; but if they are ill, this light will be a form of torture for you. Without purity of heart, you will never be able to contemplate that which is reserved exclusively for the pure of heart. You will be pushed away, you will not be admitted to this sublime vision. "Blessed are the pure in heart, for they will see God" (Ser 53,6).

Reflection Questions

What methods do I employ to remain open to hearing and seeing God's presence in my life? How do I stop from placing labels on the situations and people I see, and closing my mind to the deeper reality present there? Do I request the "eyes and heart of a child" during my prayer time so that I will be open and available to any new situation or person that God sends my way? Do I welcome and seek the hidden treasures that come my way in the new and different (and sometimes difficult) people who enter my life?

9

Mary Is a Star in the Middle of the Night

Focus Point

////////////

Mary's "yes" to God's plan of salvation is a model of human freedom in light of Divine request. Mary's "yes" was not made blindly, though. She had questions, but she also trusted God completely, and was entirely open to God's plan for her. Mary's questions concerning the possibility of God's plan never involved a lack of faith. Although Mary is the "Mother of God," she is first and foremost a servant and disciple of the Lord.

////////////

O You omnipotent good, who takes such good care
of each of us as if he were your only care, and of all
together as if each one alone? (Conf III, 11,19).

*G*od never stops calling us to him. And
God calls us through all of the events
of the universe, of history and of our lives.
Everything is the word of God, everything
asks us to return to God:

> The God of faithfulness that advised us
> to return to him ... God, to whom we
> must not completely perish; God, who
> advised us to be on watch (Sol 1,1,2–3).

But in order to draw us to him with more
strength, he put himself within our reach; he
even took our own language, even our behaviors, and never stops telling us: "Follow me!"

> The word was made flesh so that your
> wisdom, Oh God, by which you have
> created all things, might become milk for
> our infancy (Conf VII, 18,14).

Christ addresses himself to us today, just
as he addressed the shepherds and the Magi in
times past. God called the shepherds through
the angels: "To you is born this day in the city
of David a Savior, who is the Messiah, the
Lord" (Lk 2:11).

The angels were the messengers of God and everyone is an angel since every event brings us a message from God. We must know how to discern the signs, the angels that the Lord sends us and who never stop telling us: "Go to Bethlehem: a Savior is born unto you." The angels, Jesus' true messengers are like the sound of a light breeze. They invite us to life and peace.

We must have the eyes to see the stars that shine in the firmament of our lives. And it is the Virgin Mary who reveals the dispositions of our hearts to us, those which we need in order to see the light of God. The shepherds, like the Magi, "went with haste and found Mary and Joseph, and the child lying in the manger" (Lk 2:16). "On entering the house, they saw the child with Mary his mother" (Mt 2:11). Mary is always with Jesus. In order to meet Jesus, we must, then, have the same disposition as Mary, to become the Virgin Mary. We can only get close to Jesus through Mary.

> Mary is not the night, but a star in the middle of the night; it is for that reason that the birth of Jesus was indicated by a star that led the Magi, one great night, to adore the light so that, in them, "the light would shine in the middle of the darkness" (Ser 223, D, 2).

The Lord stands in front of our door and knocks. He begs for lodging in our homes. We must know to open our doors to this begging God. And it is there that the Virgin Mary takes all of her meaning for us. God invites us to welcome her. And the model, the example of what our attitude must be with respect to this invitation that the Lord makes to us, is rightfully the Virgin Mary.

Saint Luke said: "Mary was betrothed to Joseph." We must read this text in the light of the mentality of the time. Mary, according to custom, had been given in marriage without anyone ever asking her opinion on the matter. Her future had already been decided by her parents. No room for freedom was accorded to her, there was no space for personal initiatives. Betrothed to Joseph, she already knew what was awaiting her by looking around herself and seeing the way the other women of Nazareth were living.

And there, in that predetermined life, God burst in and disrupted that which man's habits wouldn't or couldn't change. He would disrupt Mary's entire life. He began by giving Mary the right to speak: God, for the first time, asked her advice, God made Mary a free woman. God fixed his gaze on her and asked her to banish all of her fears: "Do not be afraid, Mary, for you have found favor with God" (Lk 1:30).

Furthermore, he asked for an answer; he asked her for her advice. And Mary's "yes" to God's project is the possibility for each of us to also collaborate with God, to disrupt our routines and our old habits that paralyze us, that don't permit us to be what God wants from us. God comes to free us. We must also let ourselves be freed by him.

> So that we believe in Christ, dwell in his words. By dwelling there, we will truly be his disciples. For he doesn't only have twelve apostles as his disciples, he also has those who dwell in his word. This way, we will know the truth and it is the Truth, that is, Christ, the Son of God who said: "I am the truth," the truth shall set you free; it will make us free; it will emancipate us, not from the yoke of the barbarians, but from the tyranny of the devil, not from the captivity that weighs on the body, but from the iniquity that imprisons the soul. Only from somewhere else can he get this freedom for us. (Ser 134,6).

But Mary's "yes," like the "yes" of each one of us to God's project, is not made without questions. Mary didn't see clearly. The gap between the life that we lead and the life that God comes to offer us is too great. Mary "was perplexed by his words and pondered what sort of greeting this might be" (Lk 1:29). Since Mary trusted the Lord completely, she accepted God's freeing action upon her. She welcomed, into her heart, what God said to her. "Here am I, the servant of the Lord; let it be with me according to your word" (Lk 1:38). And Mary became the Mother of God. Through her faith, she gave birth to Jesus.

Mary, at the moment of the Annunciation, made us understand all of the calls that God addresses to us at the heart of our life. And what Mary experienced at the moment of the Annunciation is just what we are called to live during the course of our own lives. Mary is the example of the human who feels touched by the grace of God, who welcomes him and makes him the foundation of her life.

God intervenes in our lives and faith comes with this action by God on us. God knocks at our door and, to live faith, is to discover what God did and continues to do within us. The life of each of us is a holy story, the story of God's action upon us. Our life is strengthened by a whole series of "annunciations." And Mary teaches us what we must do to welcome them. The Virgin Mary acquaints us with the way to act with God.

Mary did the will of the Father, and that is why it is greater for her to have been a

disciple of Christ than to have been the
mother of Christ; it was a greater blessing
for her to have been a disciple of Christ
than to have been the mother of Christ.
In this way, then, Mary was happy
because, even before giving birth to him,
she carried the Master in her womb. See
if what I say is not true. Just as the Lord
went to the middle of the crowds that
followed him and performed miracles, a
woman cried: "Happy is the womb that
bore you!" (Lk 11:27). And the Lord, so
that we don't seek our happiness through
the flesh, what did he answer? "Blessed
rather are those who hear the word of
God and obey it!" (Lk 11:28). Mary was
happy then because she listened and kept
God's word; she kept the truth in her
spirit more than in the flesh of her womb.
Christ is the truth, Christ was flesh, the
Christ-Truth was in Mary's spirit, the
flesh of Christ was in her womb; but that
which is in the spirit is greater than that
which is in the flesh (Ser 72 A, 7).

However, the very first attitude that Mary
had when she was faced with the events of her
life was one of reflection. Saint Luke commented on it on numerous occasions: "... and
she pondered what sort of greeting this might
be" (Lk 1:29). "...[A]nd she treasured all these

things in her heart" (Lk 2:51). Mary was a
woman of reflection.

In the words of Zechariah, the angel had
discovered an absence of faith; he had
noticed doubt, a lack of confidence, and
the angel made him see it in himself by
removing the use of his voice, in order to
punish him for not having believed.

With respect to Mary: "How can this be,
since I am a virgin?" (Lk 1:34). Let us
remember here her vow of virginity. But
by saying "How can this be?" she sought
the means: she did not in any way doubt
the omnipotence of God. "How can this
be?" You tell me I am going to have a
son; you see that my heart is prepared,
but explain the manner to me. And the
angel, we have seen, knows that this
questioning does not exclude faith. He
sees her pondering, but still keeping her
trust in God and he does not refuse to
teach her (Ser 291,5).

She kept all of the events that she experienced
in her heart and interpreted them. Faith is not
blind obedience. Faith, when it is profoundly
experienced, is an active faith that listens to,
interprets, and lives the word of God. But faith
is never to be taken for granted. It is always

something to be built, relived and reformulated. Jesus' public life was an occasion for Mary to deepen her faith. In her, there was a confrontation between the mother who loved her son with all of her heart and the believer who followed the Savior. Each day, she had to conform herself to the choice she made at the moment of the Annunciation: recognize, in Jesus, much more than her son, the word of God who came to dwell amongst us, which we must listen to and put into practice. In Mary, there is a conflict between her maternity which possesses and her obedience to the will of God which divests.

This faith that Mary has is expressed in a very striking way in the mystery of the Visitation. The details that the Gospels offer us about the Visitation are very rich in meaning so that we can well grasp to what our life of faith commits us. "In those days Mary set out and went with haste to a Judean town in the hill country" (Lk 1:39).

At the moment of the Annunciation, Mary believed what had been said to her on behalf of the Lord. To believe means to situate our life in the space of the word of God, join our life to it; then, to leave all that belongs to us in order to be only part of God.

Mary entered Zechariah's house and greeted Elizabeth. She greeted her in the most proper and deepest meaning of the word: she brought her greetings, just as the angel had brought it to her. Mary became, then, the angel of Elizabeth's Annunciation. This is why: "When Elizabeth heard Mary's greeting, the child leaped in her womb. And Elizabeth was filled with the Holy Spirit" (Lk 1:41). God is love and love is giving of oneself. Mary, filled with God completely, totally filled with grace, could only give God.

It is interesting to state that Saint John never calls Mary by her name. He always calls her "the Mother of Jesus," then he regularly used the name of Mary to designate other women: Mary of Bethany, Mary of Magdala, and Mary of Clopas. The omission of the name Mary is, for Saint John, an intentional act. He wanted to show us the most absolute gift that Mary gave to Jesus. Mary is "the Mother of Jesus."

However, we must also state another fact that is seen in the Gospel which enlightens us about Mary's mission in our lives. In the same way as Saint John speaks of "the Mother of Jesus" in an anonymous way, he also speaks, in an anonymous way, of "the disciple that Jesus loved." And that, both of them, the mother and the disciple, were there, next to the cross. "... Standing near the cross of Jesus were his mother.... When Jesus saw his mother and the disciple whom he loved standing beside her, he said to his mother, 'Woman, here is your son.' Then he said to the disciple, 'Here is your mother.' And from that hour the disciple took her into his own home" (Jn 19:25–27).

"The disciple whom Jesus loved" is, like Mary, a person of faith and a representative of us all, of what we must be. Mary is, and must be, the mother of all Jesus' disciples, of all who welcome God's word and make it fruitful.

Saint John tells us: "And from that hour the disciple took her into his own home" (Jn 19:27). And Saint Augustine commented:

> But in whose home did John receive the mother of the Savior? There certainly were many who had told him: "We have abandoned everything to follow you," and like the others, he had heard this reply: "Whoever abandoned everything for me will receive it a hundredfold in this life." This disciple, then, had received the hundredfold of what he had left; there was enough there to receive the mother of the One who had made him the gift of it. But, at the moment when the blessed John had received this hundredfold, he was a part of a society where no one possessed anything of their own, where everything was held in common, following that which is written in the Acts of the Apostles; for the disciples of Jesus were as if they had nothing and

possessed everything. How, then, did the disciple and servant receive the mother of his Master and Lord in his home, since no one amongst the apostles possessed anything of his own? (In Joh ev, 119,3).

Thus, the expression "the disciple took her into his own home" has a much more profound meaning. The "disciple whom Jesus loved" welcomed Mary as his "mother" in that which he had that was his own as a disciple, in that which made him a true disciple, that is, in his faith. The disciple welcomed Mary as his mother in faith. And all of us, the disciples of Jesus, we must live our faith, welcome Jesus, and listen to his word as Mary welcomed it and as Mary heard it.

Each of us must be the Virgin Mary, with her same dispositions so we can meet Jesus in our lives.

Reflection Questions

In what ways is Mary a model for my faith life? Is Marian devotion a part of my regular prayer? If not, what types of devotion can I incorporate? When I pray, discerning God's will for myself, do I dialogue with the Lord as Mary did? Do I ask questions of God regarding his plan for my life? How do I respond to his will in my prayer life?

10

Hold the Stranger Back if You Want to Recognize Christ

Focus Point

////////////////

On the road to Emmaus two disciples walked with Christ but they did not recognize him. Still, they asked the stranger to stay with them that night and eat with them. Then, in the breaking of the bread, their eyes were opened. It is Jesus! In the same way, we try to see strangers with eyes of faith, seeing Jesus Christ in them. We look for the Christ in everyone — in our family members, co-workers, and in the least of our brothers and sisters.

////////////////

*Learn to love…. In proportion to how much love
grows in you, shaping you and bringing you to
resemble God … you begin to feel God
(En in ps 49,5).*

*T*oday, more than ever, we need to have
the experience of Jesus in our lives for,
outside of this experience of Jesus, there is no
true Christian life.

It is certain that Jesus promised us to always
be with us, near us: "I am with you always, to
the end of the age" (Mt 28:20).

The problem of having the experience of
Jesus or to feel him close to us then, does not
come from him, for he is always there, next to
us; the problem stems from us, for we are quite
often absent to him. Since Jesus is living and
he arose from the dead, his heart beats like
our heart. And, like his disciples, he addresses
himself even to us today to tell us: "But who do
you say that I am?" (Mt 16:15).

Who is Christ for me, for each of us? To give
an answer to that question requires us to exam-
ine our lives. We run the risk of living formulas
that are void of meaning, dried up habits and,
by this very fact we live by what we say, do, and
the fashion of the time. And then Christ comes
today putting into question all of our routines.
He never stops asking us: "And for you, who

am I?" Yet this question is, in the first place, a question about our truth, the truth of our life.

In order to answer this question correctly, we must begin by living the very same life as Jesus. To know Jesus is to be born to him: "Very truly I tell you, no one can see the kingdom of God without being born from above" (Jn 3:3); "… those who do what is true come to the light …" (Jn 3:21). We must, then, identify ourselves to him: he is our Truth.

God made us in the image of his Word. By this very fact, the Word is our truth, the model from which we have been created. Each of us, created in the image of the Word, carries his imprint within. Each of us, then, is a sacred mystery. The Word of God is present in us. Each of us, as an image of God, is an open window to God. Within ourselves, we do not have a center of gravity. Our being is then completely oriented towards God.

God attracts us to him and never stops calling us. It is not so much that we go to God that it is God drawing us to him. It is God who provokes our love. However, we do not often feel this call from God. We are in the dark. And there, God comes to our aid. He became human in order to reveal the path that leads us to him.

To want to go to God and to our truth outside of Christ, is to condemn ourselves to fail-

ure. There is no other path to go to God than
through Christ. It is imperative that we imitate
Christ. He is our truth and we must learn to
model our life after his.

> If you seek the Truth, follow the Path, for
> the Path is also the Truth. Go that way,
> you must go that way.... It is through
> Christ that you come to Christ.... To
> Christ the Lord through Christ the man;
> through the Word made flesh, to the
> Word who was close to God at the begin-
> ning (In Joh ev XIII, 4). God became a
> man so that by following a man, which
> you can do, you will reach God, which
> you couldn't do (En in ps 134,5).

We must, then, travel with Jesus. We must
live the passages of the Gospel about the disciples of Emmaus in the most intimate part of
our hearts, for this passage well explains the
most concrete and profound reality of our lives.

Christ has just died and two of his disciples,
seized with fear, leave Jerusalem. Very discouraged and sad, they return to their home in
Emmaus. Faced with so many difficulties as
we encounter around us, we also run the risk of
losing sight of Jesus and even losing our hope
of meeting him.

And we walk alone. We lead our lives in solitude. However, solitude, like isolation, means death.

After his resurrection, Jesus encountered two of his disciples on the road who were speaking about what had happened and asked them: "What are you discussing with each other while you walk along?" (Lk 24:17). This passage from the Gospel brings us a great lesson, if we have heard it. Jesus appeared, he showed himself to the eyes of the disciples, he was not recognized. The Master accompanied them on the road and it is he who is the road; but they are not yet on the true road: when Jesus met them, they had lost this road. When he lived with them, before his passion, he had truly predicted it; his suffering, his death, and his resurrection on the third day. He had proclaimed it all to them; but his death had made them lose their memories (Ser 235,1–2).

Since there remained a spark of love within them of the presence of the other, they spoke between themselves and had a discussion: "While they were talking and discussing, Jesus himself came near and went with them" (Lk 24:15). The simple fact of speaking with someone is already a great deal and that often constitutes the foundation of an act of faith. We speak to someone because we, more or less, trust them. Mistrust always renders someone silent: we expect nothing of them, not a word or a phrase.

And God starts by walking with us. He trusts us. It is he who begins the dialogue with Adam, hidden from him: "Adam, where are you?" God is a God of dialogue and communication.

And God begins by putting into question our communications. The questions that Jesus asked of his disciples, and that he continues to ask of us all, constitute a putting into question of what we seem to take for granted: " 'What are you discussing with each other while you walk along?' They stood still, looking sad" (Lk 24:17).

> "We hope, they said, that he would deliver Israel." How, disciples, did you hope, and now no longer hope? But Christ lives, and within you, hope is dead! Yes, Christ lives. But the living Christ has found the hearts of his disciples to be dead. He appeared to their eyes, and they didn't see him; he showed himself, and he remained hidden to them. If he had not shown himself how could his disciples have heard his question and answer it? He travels with them and seems to follow them, but it is he who leads them. They

see him but do not recognize him, the
text says, "for their eyes were kept from
recognizing him" (Lk 24:16) (Ser 235,2).

Jesus began by inviting them to remember.
"To remember" is to recognize God's love for
us. When the people of Israel felt drawn by the
behavior of the pagans that surrounded them
and began to adopt their ways, the Lord always
asked them to remember: "Remember, Israel,
all that the Lord has done for you." "To remember" is to rediscover the meeting that God had
with his people, the example and model for
all true meetings between God and us: "The
beginning with Moses and all the prophets, he
interpreted to them the things about himself
in all the scriptures" (Lk 24:27). Jesus helped
them "to remember." Jesus is always the same.
He continues to speak to us as he spoke to his
disciples in times past. He has not changed. We
must, then, know how "to remember."

Jesus begins by showing us that there is no
break between the Old and New Testaments:
the Word of God is one and always the
same. Everything speaks of Jesus. The Holy
Scriptures are the words that God speaks to us.
In it, God invites us to share friendship with
him. But love brings love. And the response to
God's love, which is revealed to us, manifested
in the Holy Scriptures, is always the request:
"Stay with us." The two disciples invite Jesus to

stay with them. They offered him their home,
but above all, they offered him their hearts.
And Jesus gives himself to those who invoke
him, he gives himself by breaking the bread,
the expression of his death on the cross, where
Jesus broke himself for us. In order to meet
Jesus, we must have the same experience, the
experience of the gift, the experience of love.
The disciples of Emmaus recognized Jesus by
the welcome: "… everyone who loves is born of
God and knows God" (1 Jn 4:7).

> Oh well, my brothers, when did the Lord
> want to show himself? At the breaking of
> the bread. We can be sure of that: by shar-
> ing the bread, we recognize the Lord: he
> only wanted to be recognized at that time
> because of those of us who didn't see him
> in the flesh and would still eat his flesh.
> (…) The absence of the Lord is not an
> absence. Just believe, and the one who
> you do not see is with you. When Jesus
> spoke to the disciples, they didn't have
> faith; and because they didn't believe that
> he had arisen from the dead, they didn't
> hope to be able to arise themselves from
> the dead. They had lost faith; they had
> lost hope. Dead, they walked with a liv-
> ing being. Dead, they walked with Life.
> Life walked with them, but their hearts
> had not come back to life yet. And you, if

you want life, do what they did, and you will recognize the Lord. They received the stranger: the Lord, as if he was a traveler who was going far away, but they knew to keep him. "When they came to their village, they said to him: stay here with us because it is almost evening." Hold the stranger back if you want to recognize Christ. What doubt had made you lose, hospitality will bring back. The Lord manifested his presence in the sharing of the bread (Ser 235, 3).

If we want to know Christ, then, we must have his experience, the experience of love for others. The one who loves his neighbors, loves God. Sharing and charity make us know Christ. Christ comes amongst us when we go to others.

Reflection Questions

Do I seek out the image of Christ in everyone I meet, or do I write some people off simply because of the way that they're dressed, or the way they talk, or because they hold a different opinion from the one I present? Do I encounter each stranger I meet with a sense of welcome, a spirit of charity, ready to learn from this new person and perceive God at work inside of this stranger?

11

Lord, Lend Me Your Light!

Focus Point

//////////////

Christ healed the rift between God and all of us when he died for our sins on the cross. Christ continues to heal us, though. He is the Doctor and we are his patients. He heals our blind eyes and our blind hearts so that we might see him more clearly, know him in a deeper way, and strengthen our love for him. If we are hurting, we must call out to Jesus and implore that he heal us. We must put all of our hope and trust into Jesus Christ.

//////////////

May all of our concerns in this world then, be to heal this eye of the heart which makes us see God (Ser 88,5).

*C*hrist is the Way and the Path that we must follow in order to meet God. In order to go to God, we must follow the road that he took to come to us. We must, then, walk in Jesus' path.

In all that he did, he taught us how we must live here on earth (Ser 75,2).

The imitation of Christ, then, is imperative for us all. We have been created in his image. He is the model for what we are and what we must do. He is the Shape to which we must conform our lives.

But Jesus is much more for us than the model for our lives. He is also the Savior, the Redeemer. He came to save the sinners that we are. The reason for his Incarnation was not simply to offer us some precepts or a few examples of life; it is, above all, to offer us salvation.

"The saying is sure and worthy of full acceptance, that Christ Jesus came into the world to save sinners — of whom I am the foremost ..." (1 Tim 1:15). Take away the ill and the wounds: there is no longer a need for doctors. If the great Doctor came down from heaven, it is because a great patient was lying across the face of the universe. That great patient was the human race (Ser 175,1).

In all of Christ's names, the one that calls him the Doctor is, for Saint Augustine, one of the most important. He saw all of the work of the Redemption as a healing, for we have an illness at the very depths of our hearts. We are wounded at the most intimate part of our being. We are all blind to the light of God, deaf to his words and paralyzed in the face of his call to come to him.

> Don't despair, you are blind, come close to him and you will be healed; you are blind, come close to him and you will be illuminated. You who are healthy, give thanks; you who are ill, run to him to be healed; … run to the Doctor, implore the Doctor, you will find him everywhere (Ser 176,5).

And Jesus, himself, offers us the conditions that we all must fulfill in order to approach him and allow ourselves to be healed by him. We are the sick who are spoken about in the Gospel. Their behaviors are our own. We are, then, the blind of Jericho who are spoken about in the Gospel of Matthew (20:29–34).

Jesus was on the road to Jerusalem. Jerusalem would be the place where he would suffer his passion, his death on the cross, and where he will arise from the dead. Jerusalem is the fulfillment of Easter. Jesus turned his life into an Easter, a road. Jesus traveled towards the cross, but the cross is the supreme revelation of his love for us. On the cross, Jesus deprived himself of everything, he had nothing left. That is the most perfect expression of his passage amongst us. Jesus passed as a gift passes: from hand to hand.

Yet, to travel, to pass, inevitably requires a certain change of scenery and this is the mortifying removal of the security of everything that is familiar to us. And Jesus, by his life as by his death, teaches us to always be on the road, to never stop or set ourselves up at this place or the next. Our condition on earth is to be pilgrims, to become gifts like Christ, he who is the ultimate gift.

What does it mean: the Lord passed by? He told us; he did transitory works, and it is by these transitory works that our faith is practiced. But the Word of God, through which everything was done, is not the only object of our faith; for if, by remaining always in the form of God, equal to God, he did not negate himself by taking on the form of a servant, the blind would not notice his passage and not have cried out to him; but while he

did these transitory works, that is to say,
he humbled himself, by making himself
obedient all the way to death and a death
on the cross, the two blind men shouted
even louder: "Have mercy on us, Lord,
Son of David" (Ser 88,11).

Upon entering Jericho, Jesus met two
blind men. They were also beggars. They
had absolutely nothing to call their own in
this world. They were on the side of the road.
Jesus passed, they were seated. Jesus is the
Light, they are blind. However, they come to
learn that it was Jesus who was passing. And
it was simply their poverty that made them feel
the presence of Jesus next to them. Poverty is
certainly a detachment from material things,
but it is, above all, a disposition of heart: it is
the heart that is offered, the heart that gives of
itself. This poverty of heart that allows us to
see Jesus is humility. Humility makes us discover the presence of God next to us. It is the
condition that is absolutely necessary in order
to recognize Jesus as he passes. It is the poor
and the humble who recognize Jesus.

The blind men "heard that Jesus was passing by, they shouted 'Lord, Have mercy on us,
Son of David!' The crowd sternly ordered them
to be quiet" (Mt 20:30–31). In the first place,
there was a crowd that wanted to prevent them
from calling to Jesus. We are all surrounded by

a crowd of noises which seek, by all means, to stop us from calling to the Lord.

It is in the middle of the crowd that they shouted and the Lord heard them. You are also in the midst of sinners and sensualists who are all devoted to the pleasures of the times, you must cry out so that the Lord can heal you (Ser 88,17).

We do not, then, have the right to be discouraged. In the midst of the discouragement that wracks the heart, the Lord approaches us to tell us: "What do you want me to do for you?" (Mt 20:32). Jesus never stops passing next to us and he only seeks to help us. He simply asks us to call him, to cry out to him for he will always come to the one who calls him and who is truly in need of him. We must, then, today, more than ever, shout and shout loudly to Jesus.

In our trials as in our solitudes, Jesus asks us only one thing: to put all of our hope in him, for he is the only one who can heal our hearts. We are all blind people and poor people and we all need to be healed of our mistrusts and discouragements.

Jesus asked the blind men: "What do you want me to do for you?" What would our answer be if Jesus asked us this question today? What do we expect from Jesus? Yes, the blind men answered: "Lord, let our eyes be opened"

(Mt 20:33). For those who are blind, it is completely normal to ask for sight. But for Jesus, at
least apparently, that didn't seem right to him.
The blind men could have well asked him for
money; for they were also beggars. Jesus put
them into the disposition to be conscious of
what they asked. He wants us to be very conscious of what we ask of him. Jesus teaches us
not only to pray, to cry out to him, but also to
be true in our requests. By expressing our tru-
est desires, he helps us to be true to ourselves.

> But why does he ask us to pray, him,
> the one who knows what we need even
> before we ask him for it? The question
> could be troubling, if we don't under-
> stand that our Lord and our God want
> not what would be manifested to him by
> our will — that he couldn't ignore — but
> what our desire practices in our prayer —
> the one who allows us to receive the gift
> that he reserves for us (Ep 130,17–18).

The blind men asked for sight. Jesus would
give them more: faith and salvation. And when
the crowd was almost ready to leave Jesus, the
two blind men having become sighted, also
became believers: "Immediately they regained
their sight and followed him" (Mt 20:34). They
would follow Jesus on the road to Jerusalem,
on the road that would lead him to his passion,

to the cross. They took the road that the others just refused. The two blind men, from that moment on, saw only Jesus.

Such is the Light in which we must recognize the situation in which we find ourselves. Like the blind men, we have to accept to be seen by Jesus just as we are; we have to accept to give ourselves to him, so that he can accomplish, within us, what appears to be impossible: to find the sight of our hearts again.

But the healed blind man did not soon enter onto the path that all of his relatives, neighbors, and friends began to make for him; the experts of the times stated the opposite: "What foolishness has come over you? You do too much; aren't the others Christians? Yes, pure foolishness, true madness drives you!" It was with cries such as these that the crowd sought to mask the cries of the blind men; the other crowd wanted to prevent the blind men from shouting but couldn't drown out their voices. May they understand what they have to do, those who want to be healed. There are those who honor God with their lips and whose hearts are far from him. Those whose contrite hearts are obedient to the Lord alone keep themselves on the journey (Ser 88, 13).

In this passage of the Gospel, we meet all of the elements that we need so that the light, and with the light, hope, comes to be born in our hearts. We must recognize that we are people who are only partially sighted, that we are poor and that we are seated for we are afraid to follow Jesus on the road to Jerusalem. Our lack of hope comes from the deformed reality we have created, and from the fact that we are only partially sighted about reality and from the idea that we do not know how to see Jesus as he passes by. It is a deformation of our vision. Our heart is blinded. We must, like the blind men, shout to Jesus. We must not pay attention to the interior and exterior noises that drown out our voices and prevent us from calling to Jesus.

Reflection Questions

Do I cry out to Jesus in prayer that he might heal my blind heart? Do I pray that I might be freed from the illusions that serve as my reality, that do little more than restrict my world-view to a narrow, angry, cold outlook? Do I recognize the need for emotional healing in my life? Do I see a need for healing between me and a brother or a sister, a friend I have neglected to keep in touch with, or someone whom I have had a falling out? Can I pray to God that he lend his grace to this troubled situation and heal it as only he can?

12

The Church,
the Body of Christ

Focus Point

///////////////

We are to have the same mind as Jesus; the very
same outlook on life. Because we are the Church,
the Body of Christ the Head, we are to continue
his ministry on earth as we await the final days.
We are to spread the Good News, promote healing, and unity. We are to bring everyone into the
fold under Christ the Head. The Body and the
Head are one being, says Augustine, Christ and
his Church are the "total Christ."

///////////////

Let us love the Lord our God, let us love his Church:
he, like a father, she, like a mother; he, like a master,
she, like a servant, for we are the children of this
very servant. Let us all reach a common agreement
then that God is the father and the Church is our
mother (En in ps 88, 11,14).

*G*od asks us to be perfect as he is perfect.
God asks us to be love as he is love. To
help us fulfill this commandment, he became
human, just like us, with the exception of sin
(Heb 4:15). He became human to show us, with
his life and teachings, the road that leads us
to our perfection, the road of love, the road of
charity. Christ never stopped telling us: "I am
the way, and the truth, and the life" (Jn 14:6).
We must all go to Christ, follow him, and put
all of our trust in him. In Christ, we will meet
our perfection and truth.

It is certain that we must not have the same
historical behaviors as Jesus, but we must have
the same motivations in our hearts as he did.
Saint Paul tells us: "Let the same mind be in
you as was in Christ Jesus" (Phil 2:5).

Christ is never far from us and, as such, we
don't have to search very far in order to meet
him. He is living. Today, Jesus' presence in
the midst of us is the Church, it is the "total
Christ."

Our Lord, Jesus Christ is man in his totality, head and body. In this man, we know who is the head: it is the one who was born of the Virgin Mary. (...) His body is the Church (En in ps 90, 11,1).

It is certain that Jesus' disciples saw only the head of the "total Christ," just as we, today, see only his body, the Church; but the head and the body make up only one single and unique person. This union between Christ and the Church is so close that it filled Saint Augustine with admiration and fervor and he didn't hesitate to say that we are not only with Christ, but that we are Christ himself.

The mystery of the Church has its basis in the mystery of the Incarnation. Saint Augustine used the same expressions to speak of the Incarnation of Christ and the reality of the Church. In the womb of the Virgin Mary, the Word of God was united to the flesh. And with this same flesh, joined himself to the Church and, from that moment on, the Word became the "total Christ."

The Word was made flesh and it dwells among us. To this flesh, the Church is joined and it is the total Christ, head and body (In Joh ep, 1,2).

The Church was born with the Incarnation of Christ and, in the same way, we must approach the light of this mystery. The Church is the revelation of God's love for us. God reveals his love to us and unites us to him.

It is in his Son that the Father loves us because it is in him that he chose us before the creation of the world. The one who loves the only Son necessarily loves those who have been adopted by and for him…. The one who loves the Son can't prevent himself from loving the body of his Son, and the only reason that the Father loves them is because of the love he has for the Son. (…) With respect to us, he loves us because we are the body of the Son whom he loves; and so that we can become his body, he loved us even before we existed (In Joh ev 110,5–6).

We are both the Church and with the Church, for we are its body, which is a fact that can't be understood outside of the context of God's love for us. It is this love that God has for us that is the foundation of Christ's Incarnation and, at the same time, the Church.

This communion between God and us all is created by and through the Holy Spirit. The Holy Spirit plays the same role with respect to the Church as it does with us, its body.

The soul is to the human body as the Holy Spirit is to the body of Christ; it

accomplishes, in the entire Church, that
which the soul does in all of the parts of
a single body (Ser 267,4).

The Holy Spirit, the soul of the Church, is a
spirit of union and communion and those who
receive it can only live with respect to others.
What it does with the Father and the Son in
the Holy Trinity, it does equally between the
members of the Church. Communion, then, is
the first characteristic of the Church and the
clearest manifestation of our membership in it.

The Holy Spirit, then, is the one who created the Church. It is the gift from the Father to
the Son and from the Son to the Father and it
comes to us, for the first time, at the moment of
our baptism. The Holy Spirit shares its nature
of giving with whomever receives it.

It is because the Father and the Son are
in communion that they want to have a
communion with us, and through this
gift, gather all that is theirs together in
unity, that is, the Holy Spirit, God himself
and the gift of God. It is in him that we
have been reconciled with the Divinity
and in whom we rejoice (Ser 71,18).

The Holy Spirit is the spirit of the ecclesiastical community and it comes to us as a func-
tion of how much we go to others. We are in
communion with God by and in our ecclesias-

tical communion. We are also closest to God in the Church.

Christian perfection is reached through union and communion with God. Only the members that are given life by the Holy Spirit are able to live the life of Jesus. Unity, then, to the body of Christ, is an essential attribute of the Church.

> We dwell in the Lord when we are his body and he dwells in us when we are his temple. So that we will be his body, unity gives us structure. What does unity give as a structure if not charity? The Apostle asked: "And where does the charity of God come from?" "The charity of God," he replied, "had been spread in our hearts by the Holy Spirit who had been given to us ..." (In Joh ev 27,6).

Charity is the health of the Church and it is that which makes the Church a community: the Church is in perfect communion with the plurality of the members of which it is comprised. But this perfection of the Church, the perfect peace between its different members, will never be shared with us in this world. Saint Augustine made a clear distinction between the future Church and the Church of this world:

> There is one Church here on earth and one up above, one made up by the

entirety of the faithful, the other by the entirety of the angels. But the Lord of the angels descended to the Church on earth and, whereas he served us, the angels served him (En in ps 137,4).

The future Church is the Church of heaven, there, where there no longer is death, tears, or worries. However, in the Church of this world, there are dissensions and divisions: there is sin. The Church, being holy, keeps the sinners that we are in its heart; it is a Church that is moving forward, on a pilgrimage towards its fulfillment in heaven.

However, the Church of heaven and the one on earth are not two Churches, but two aspects of the same and single unique Church. The Church of today, the Church of this world is the Body of Christ whose holiness is not stained by the sinful members of it that we are. Even if it is poor and sinful, it is not separated from the Church in heaven. Each of us, in spite of our spiritual poverty, are truly parts of Christ's body, we are united to God. And we must work to build the Church of this world, to make it perfect. It is our mission. The perfection of the Church is the fulfillment, in this world, of the redemptive mission of Christ. In order to fulfill this mission in our world, we must increase, more and more, the union with Christ, the union of us all with Christ. And that which unites us with Christ and each other is pre-cisely the Holy Spirit, charity.

A part of a body has a better chance at good health if it not separated from the whole body; for if it is wounded, the health of the other parts comes to help it; if, to the contrary, the parts separate themselves from each other, from where and by where could health reach them? (Ser 62, A, 7).

It is certain that Christ is only accessible to us today in and through the Church. The exact amount of our love for Christ is given to us in our love for the Church. For Saint Augustine, we must not have any greater love than the one we have for the Church. The love of the Church must pass before all other loves; it is even the criteria of discernment to know God's will for us. To know the requirements of the Church is to know God's will for us.

Reflection Questions

Do I recognize myself as a member of the Body of Christ on earth, and am I aware of the responsibilities as a member of the Church that continues the ministry of Jesus Christ on this earth? What talents has God graced me with that I might serve his Church as a unique member of his Body? In an effort to take on the mind and outlook of Jesus, what types of awareness prayers might I employ in broadening my current world-view?

13

The Eucharist, the Sacrament of the Church

Focus Point

Sin is the source of human division, and division from God. Just as a baker mixes all of the ingredients that form bread into one loaf, so does Jesus unite all divided sinners into his divine body, the Bread of Life, and here shares the life of God with us. Jesus Christ offers his life on our behalf, as we as the Church, the Body of Christ, offer our lives to God as well during the Mass and into our daily lives. We are the Body of Christ. Amen. Amen.

So that you are not dispersed, eat the One who is your connection (Ser 228 B).

*M*editation on the mystery of the Eucharist takes a place of great importance in the life and thoughts of Saint Augustine. It should hold this same important place in our lives, for the Eucharist is the sacrament of the Body of Christ. But the Body of Christ is not simply the body of Jesus who suffered the passion and a death on the cross for us; it is also the total Body of Christ, that is, the Church. The Church is truly the Body of Christ, and the Eucharist is its sacrament.

The Eucharist, the sacrament of the Church, represents it and builds it. The Eucharist, then, is the sign of unity of all Christians with Christ and between us all. But the Eucharist creates this unity at the same time as it creates fraternal charity.

> The faithful know that it is the Body of Christ if they don't neglect to be the Body of Christ. May they become the Body of Christ if they want to live of the Spirit of Christ. The Body of Christ only lives of the Spirit of Christ. Understand, my brothers, what I have just said ... do you, consequently, want to live of the Spirit of Christ? Be in the Body of Christ.... That is why the apostle Paul explained what

this bread was in this manner: "We are a single bread, a single body, we who are numerous ..." (In Joh ev 26,13).

The Eucharist is a sign, but a sign of the Church's most profound reality. It helps us discover the mystery of the Body of Christ: the unity of all Christians with Christ and between us all. All of us, united to Christ, form only one single body with him. We are the parts of the Body of Christ and it is the Holy Spirit who unites us.

Only the love of the Holy Spirit, spread into our hearts, is able to gather us, who may be separated by our interests, into a community. And it is the Body of Christ, spirited by the Holy Spirit that the Eucharist signifies. The Eucharist is the sign of unity of the Church.

Look how you have become one single body. How does one make bread? We beat it and mold it; we moisten it with water and we bake it; by moistening it with water, we purify it; by cooking it, we harden it.... But just as the grains of wheat, that were once isolated, then ground, and finally reunited into a single mass by moistening, becoming a single loaf of bread, in the same manner, the body of Christ becomes one through unity and charity. Yet the similarity between the body of Christ and the grains of wheat is also found between the blood and grape seeds, for the wine comes from the press and, that which was separated in the multitude of seeds, flows in the unity of the same wine. In this way, then, we find the mystery of unity in the bread and wine (Ser 227 A).

But the Eucharist is much more than the sign of unity and peace of the Church; it creates that unity. The Eucharist creates what it signifies.

The Eucharist is the fulfillment of the mystery of the Incarnation. God who is love so loved the world that he gave us his Son (see Jn 3:16). Jesus is the revelation of the love of the Father for us and he revealed this love in a way that was so astounding on the cross. On the cross, he had nothing left because he had given everything to us. He died to give us life. At the Last Supper, at the institution of the Eucharist, Jesus assumed his death on the cross. The cross delivers the key to us that allows us to understand the Eucharist. In the Eucharist, Jesus continues to live the mystery of his death and the mystery of our redemption. By our redemption, Jesus freed us from sin. Sin, all sin, is the source of division. And Jesus, by his death, by the Eucharist, "gathered into one all the dispersed children of God" (Jn 11:52).

The Redemption, and by its very existence, the Eucharist, has, as its goal, the unity of us all, which it does for, in the Eucharist, Jesus shares the very life of God with us — a life of unity and love. Each day in the Eucharist, Christ redoes what sin undoes in our lives.

Christ is truly present in the Eucharist: the bread and the wine are truly the body and blood of Christ, and they are given to us to participate in the life of God. The one who eats his body and drinks his blood unites himself with Christ and, with the others, makes up one single body, the body of Christ.

> This bread that you see on the altar, sanctified by the Word of God, is the body of Christ. This cup, or rather, what is contained in this cup, sanctified by the Word of God, is the blood of Christ. By these elements, the Lord Christ wanted to entrust us with his body and his blood which he shed for us in remission of our sins. If you have received them properly, you are what you have received; for the apostle said: "Because there is one bread, we who are many are one body, for we all partake of the one bread" (1 Cor 10:17). That is how the mystery of the Lord's table is explained ... (Ser 227).

That is why Saint Augustine asked us to get closer to the Eucharist, so that we can receive the body and blood of Christ, for the Eucharist is the bread of unity. In us, it produces what it signifies. It introduces us into God's life, the life of the Trinity where the Father lives in unity with the Son in the love of the Holy Spirit. To receive the body of Christ is to share the very life of the Son and enter, by this action, into the very mystery of the Trinity.

> Receive and eat the body of Christ, after which you have become parts of the body of Christ. Receive and drink the blood of Christ. (...) Since you possess life in him, you will be with him in a single flesh.... That is what the Scriptures proclaimed and the apostle repeated: "The two will become one flesh" (Eph 5:31). He added, this mystery of Christ and the Church is great. (...) (Ser 228 B).

In the Eucharist, Christ continues to offer himself to the Father for us. But the Eucharist, the sacrament of the Body of Christ, is also the sacrifice of the whole Church. In it, the whole Church offers itself to the Father.

> The true sacrifice is all works which contribute to uniting us with God.... Consequently, man, blessed by the name of God and devoted to God, in as much

as he dies to the world in order to live in
God, is a sacrifice (De civ Dei 10,6).

And we, the members of the Church,
parts of the body of Christ, must relive the
Eucharist in our own lives. Our life will truly
be Christian and holy in proportion to how
much it is eucharistic.

So that our life is eucharistic, we must fulfill
the word of Jesus: "Do this in memory of me."
Too often we run this risk of limiting the "this"
to reproduce the rites, the gestures and words
of Jesus at the moment of the institution of
the Eucharist. It is much more. "This" is what
Jesus "lived" at the Last Supper. He invites us
to enter into his eucharistic act: to take our
lives in hand, break ourselves and agree to die
to all that is an obstacle to charity, to give ourselves in communion in order to become the
bread of unity and peace for all people. "Do
this in memory of me": Jesus invites us to enter
into his eucharistic act, to make ourselves the
Eucharist.

The Eucharist, then, is the sacrament of
the Church: it signifies the true reality of the
Church and realizes it, but it also helps us to
live our membership to the Church in perfection.

If, then, you are the body of Christ and its
members, it is your mystery that is placed

on the Lord's table, and it is your mystery that you receive. To what you are, you respond "Amen," and by responding, you become part of it. In fact, you hear; "the body of Christ"; and you reply: "Amen." Be part of Christ, so that your "Amen" is true (Ser 272).

Reflection Questions

Is the celebration of the Eucharist at the center of my life? In what ways can I help to foster a devotion to the Body and Blood of Christ? Perhaps attend a Benediction of the Blessed Sacrament at my local parish? As I participate in the Mass am I consciously making the effort to offer up all that I am (with Jesus, as he does) in praise of and thanksgiving to the Father?

14

The Virgin Mary, the Mother and Model of the Church

Focus Point

////////////

Mary serves as the model of faith for us, the people of God. Mary receives the Word of God and allows herself to be transformed by it. Like Mary's virginity was consecrated to God in fidelity, so is the Church a virgin through faith, placing all trust in the Lord. And just as Mary the Mother nourished the Infant Jesus, so does the Church nourish its members with love, compassion, and faith.

////////////

Mary believed, and what she believed was realized in her. Let us believe also so that what she realized is also beneficial to us (Ser 215,4).

*T*he Virgin Mary is the clearest and also the most profound expression of the mystery of the Church. When we get closer to the Church, we get closer to Mary. Mary is the light of the Church.

Mary's very first virtue, according to Saint Augustine, was virginity. Virginity is the human way of living the experience of the Church in heaven. She gives birth, in an original way, to the life in heaven, in order to reveal it or manifest it to all. She is like a type of sacrament, for she signifies the life in heaven and, at the same time, she lives it.

Virginity is to propose, in a corruptible flesh, a perpetual incorruptibility (De virg 13,12).

Virginity makes the lives of the angels and the morals of heaven appear to mankind (De virg 54,54).

And it is the mystery of the Incarnation that allows us to understand the deepest meaning of virginity. In the mystery of the Incarnation, human nature sanctifies itself by its union with the Word of God and it reveals the Word of

God to everyone. Through virginity, the virginity of the body reveals and manifests the virginity of heart. Virginity of heart is to live in a total and absolute union with God.

> It isn't from itself, but from being consecrated to God that virginity gets its honor. We keep it in the flesh, but it is for a religious or a spiritual devotion that we keep it, in such a way that the virginity of the flesh itself is spiritual, dedicated, and kept like it is by continence and piety (De virg 8,5).

Virginity, then, is a certain way to live the mystery of the Incarnation in our lives. Virginity, like the mystery of the Incarnation, is the result of love and humility.

Where there is a lack of love or charity, virginity is impossible. It was charity that led God to become human, it is love that brings us to virginity. Virginity, then, is an expression of love.

And Mary offered herself completely to God in order to become his sign, his word for all people. Mary consecrated herself completely to God. God was the only one for her. That is the foundation of her vow of virginity.

> Mary consecrated her virginity to God when she again ignored what she was called to conceive so that, if she realized the life in heaven in her earthly mortal

body, that would be in virtue of her vow, not in virtue of a precept, by an all loving choice, not through the necessity to obey (De virg 4,4).

And Saint Augustine insisted on this consecration of Mary's virginity. Mary's total gift to God would be founded on faith and it would be faith that opened Mary to maternity. Mary will be, at the same time, both the Virgin and the Mother. It is the greatest miracle of the entire Gospel. By contemplating on it, Saint Augustine fell into admiration and praise.

Let us then speak of this event. But are we able to? An angel proclaimed it: the Virgin listened, believed, and conceived. She had faith in her heart and Christ in her womb. A virgin, she conceives, who would not be astonished at that? A virgin, she gave birth, be even more astonished that, having given birth, she was still a virgin! (Ser 196,1).

And Mary became the Mother of God through faith. Faith is much more than admitting that a group of doctrines or teachings are true. Faith is knowing how to welcome the Word of God and allowing ourselves to be transformed by it. Mary lived her entire life in the most complete fidelity to the Word of God.

Virginity, firstly, consists in the integrity of faith. Virginity is a consecration to God, a positive personal relationship with him. It has its foundation in the heart: it is the heart that gives itself, that offers itself completely to the Lord.

Mary's virginity is the most precious fruit of her love and fidelity to God. But God's love always brings with it human love. There are not two commandments: love God, love your neighbor, but only one unique commandment: "The commandment we have from him is this: those who love God must love their brothers and sisters" (1 Jn 4:21). And Mary became the Mother of God and the Mother of us all.

The Blessed Virgin Mary conceived, through faith, the One who she also gave birth to through faith. When the angel proclaimed that she would have a son, she asked the angel how that would happen, since she had not ever known a man. She only saw a single way of conceiving and giving birth, of which she had never had the experience, but which she knew through the example of other women, according to the laws of nature, that is, through the union of a man and a woman. The angel then replied to her: "The Holy Spirit will come upon you and the power of the Most High will overshadow you; therefore the child to be born will be holy; he will be called Son of God" (Lk 1:35). After these words from the angel, Mary, filled with faith, by conceiving Christ in her soul before conceiving him in her womb, said to him: "Here am I, the servant of the Lord; let it be with me according to your word" (Lk 1:38).... Mary believed the words of the angel, and she lived to fulfill, within herself, what she had believed. Let us also believe, with her, that we can gather the fruits of this mystery (Ser 215,4).

Mary is the Mother and Model of the Church. Furthermore, she is its most perfect fulfillment. To meet Mary is to meet the Church. The mystery of the Church becomes the light in Mary. The Church, like Mary, is both a virgin and a mother.

The Church is, first of all, a virgin through faith. Virginity is to keep the fidelity to the Lord intact. And the Church, following Mary's example, puts all of its trust in the Lord.

And like Mary, the Church is both a virgin and a mother. Fidelity to God's will necessarily led it to serve all people. Just as Mary traveled to serve Elizabeth after the Annunciation, since then, we can say that Mary is always traveling on our roads in order to bring us salvation. The Church is also traveling in order to grant us God's life. It never stops granting us faith and nourishing us with it. The Church makes the life of Jesus incarnate in us and it nourishes it through the Scriptures and the sacraments. The Church is our mother in faith and it nourishes us as children of God. God grants us his life through the Church.

Christ came to save us and he saves us today through and by the Church. Mary is both Virgin and Mother, the Church is both Virgin and Mother. Everything is oriented towards God and towards us.

> The Church is a virgin. You could per-haps say to me: if it is a virgin, how does it give birth? I reply: it is a virgin and it gives birth. It imitates Mary who gave birth to the Savior. Would Mary not be a virgin, she who gave birth, while remaining a virgin? It is the same for the Church: it gives birth and is a virgin; and all things considered, it gave birth to Christ; for those who are baptized are part of him. The apostle said, you are the body of Christ, you are a part of him. If, then, it gives birth to parts of Christ, its resemblance to Mary could not be more complete (Ser 213,8).

The Church is not an abstract reality. It is each of us in union with the other parts of the Body of Christ. By that very fact, Mary is the

Mother and the model of each of us. She is the most perfect fulfillment of what is and what our lives must be each day. She makes us discover the most profound meaning for our existence. We must, then, know how to meet in her.

Thus, there is no Annunciation without a Visitation, there is no longer a virginity without a maternity. The union with God leads us to a union with others. Each of us must, then, be an example of Mary, virgin and mother. Everyone oriented towards God, bowing to others.

> All of the faithful members of the Church, no matter what order they belong to, have offered to Christ what his grace has allowed them to offer. In this way, then, since Jesus Christ is the truth, peace and justice, conceive of him through faith, bring him up to date on your works so that your heart will make, through the law of Jesus Christ, what the womb of Mary did to give him his body. (...) Mary gave birth to Christ, and the Church gave birth to you. For it is a virgin and a mother: a mother by the womb of charity, a virgin by the inviolability of faith and piety ... (Ser 192, 2).

Mary is the Mother and model of the Church; she is the Mother and model of us all. Mary reveals the most profound meaning of the Church and the mystery of our lives to us. We must, then, know how to meet in her. Her vocation is the vocation of the Church; her vocation is our own vocation. Mary teaches us to live our vocation.

Reflection Questions

In what ways do I try to emulate Mary as Virgin and Mother? Do I devote my fidelity entirely to God the Father? Do I pray on this, and welcome his will into my life? In what ways do I nourish the members of the Church? Do I participate in any parish outreach groups, the Legion of Mary, communion calls to shut-ins, and so on? What other methods of parish outreach might suit my individual gifts and talents?

15

Hope,
a Famished Love

Focus Point

///////////////

Our hope is not "pie-in-the-sky," vain dreaming.
Our hope is the source of life, and this hope is
constantly awakened by Jesus. The foundation
of our hope is love, a hunger for Jesus and all
that he promises us. The hope to be with him in
heaven fills our hearts each day. Our hope moves
us to love, to gather hurt and broken people into
one body, under Christ the Head, so that all will
be united to him in love.

///////////////

*My hope lies completely and uniquely in the
immense greatness of your mercy. Grant what you
command and command what you will (Conf X,
29,40).*

*Hope for nothing but your God so that the Lord,
your God, will be your sole hope (En in ps 39,7).*

*T*oday, and perhaps more than ever, we
need to meditate about hope, for we
truly need to give meaning to our lives. Today,
people feel wounded in their hearts. The sick-
ness that we suffer from today is desperation.
We are convinced that everything is up to fate
and that we can do nothing to change it. Our
era is an era of depression.

And there, in the midst of this despair that
the heart feels mired in, the Lord knocks at our
door to tell us: "I am the resurrection and the
life" (Jn 11:25). Jesus invites us to relive the
mystery of his Easter, to leave our fears and
refuges behind and to face fate. The Holy Spirit
is not a timid spirit, but a strong one (see 2 Tim
1:7), and it is he who fills our hearts with hope
and life, on the condition that we put all of our
trust in him. It is he alone who makes hope
flow in our hearts.

"Hope in the Lord." It is not a false being
in whom you are placing your hope, or
someone who could be deceitful.... He

is omnipotent, someone who does what he promises, he is truthful and faithful. Hope in the Lord and act with courage. (...) By being hopeful in the Lord, you will come to possess him, you will possess the one in whom you will have hoped (En in ps 26,11,23).

Hope is a force that is found hidden between the most intimate folds of our hearts. It is the source of life. The person who does not have hope, stops living. The danger that menaces hope is always the death of desire. When that happens, we don't want to continue on, we stop and look back.

Do you remember the woman from Lot? She was already on the road and delivered from Sodom and she looked back, she stayed there; she became a pillar of salt (see Gen 19:26). (...) Consider this woman who looked back and, following Paul's example, advance towards what is ahead of you. What does it mean when we say to not look back? The apostle told us that it is, "forgetting what lies behind" (Phil 3:13) (En in ps 139,2).

Hope is to travel with Jesus. We are on the road and Jesus never stops telling us: "Come, follow me." Jesus asks us to travel with him.

He always awakens hope. We must, then, let ourselves be guided by him, for allowing ourselves to be guided by Jesus is to live in hope.

It is certain that we will find our road to be a very difficult one. We walk through life as the boat navigates the sea. On the sea, the boat encounters many storms and the waves wash over it. Our life is the same; there are storms and failures. We become discouraged. We run the risk of losing all hope, but without hope, life is impossible.

In the midst of our difficulties and our solitudes, Christ is always there, close to us. We must simply know how to awaken our trust in him.

"And while they were sailing, he (Jesus) fell asleep ... the boat was filling with water and they were in danger" (Lk 8:23). We also navigate on a lake which lacks neither wind nor storms; daily temptations of the world almost submerge our boat. Where do they come from if Jesus isn't asleep? If Jesus wasn't asleep in you, you would not have these storms; you would enjoy a great interior calm because Jesus watches with you. What does it mean: Jesus sleeps? Your faith in Jesus is asleep. The storms on the lake rise up.... What will you do to be saved? Awaken Jesus in you and say to him: "Master, we are perishing" (Lk 8:24). Everything that is uncertain on the lake troubles us and we perish. But he awakens, that is, your faith comes back.... Turn your back on what befalls you and turn your face to what remains ... (En in ps 25, 11, 4).

Jesus plants the seeds of hope in our hearts, for hope is a gift that is granted to us. We can't give hope to ourselves; we receive it from God. Hope is like a seed that begins to grow so that it will produce fruit. Hope always gives hope for someone or something.

But hope, like the seed that is scattered on the earth, needs to be welcomed in our hearts so that it will take root. We must also care for it, for it runs the risk of being choked out. Hope is a small flame that requires much vigilance.

"His lamp shone throughout the night." "No one after lighting a lamp puts it under the bushel basket" (Mt 5:15). You light my lamp, Lord. Our lamp is our hope. In its light, all mankind works: all that he does that is good is guided by hope. This lamp also shines in the night. If we hope for what we cannot see, it is because the night still lasts in us. (...) So that we are not discouraged in the midst of darkness and to wait patiently for what we are hoping for and not seeing,

may our lamp remain lit throughout the
night. God grants us his word each day
and never stops filling our lamp with oil
so that it never goes out (Ser 37,11).

The foundation of hope is love, for hope is
much more than hoping for something, it is,
above all, to hope for someone. God loves us
and never stops inviting us to go to him and
meet him. But so that hope flows from our
hearts, it is not enough for God to love us and
offer us his love. We must also know how to
welcome this love that God has for us.

Hope, then, is a search — not a search
within a void just for the sake of searching. In
this search, we seek God. For us, to hope is to
identify ourselves with Jesus. Life, like Jesus'
mission, is only a seed that grows from day to
day until it reaches its bounty.

"Father, I desire that those also, whom
you have given me, may be with me
where I am ..." (Jn 17:24). The Lord Jesus
inspires his disciples here with the greatest hope that could be conceived. Listen
and rejoice in what this hope gives you, in
that which brings us, not to love this life,
but to endure it. (...) Listen, believe, hope,
and desire what he says: "Father, I desire
that those also, whom you have given
me, may be with me where I am...." It

is impossible for the all-powerful Father
not to fulfill the desire expressed by his
all-powerful Son ... (In Joh ev 111,1).

The lack of hope and the presence of despair
in our lives have their roots in forgetting Jesus.
We always run the risk of losing sight of Jesus.
When that happens, we put all of our hope in
the numerous idols that we give ourselves. Our
idols are like the Canaan divinities of the people of Israel. But Israel, thanks to the prophets,
rediscovered its confidence in the future. We
must never forget that our hope is not born in
our hearts, but in God's heart, and God continues to tell us: "... those who wait for me shall
not be put to shame" (Isa 49:23).

Hope is truly hope in proportion to the very
fact that it is alive, that is, creative. And our
hope will be alive if our love for God is true.
Love gives life to our hearts. It is hope that
gives birth to God in our hearts.

Reflection Questions

Do I possess a feeling, a mood of hope each
day? What is the basis of this hope? If I am not
hopeful, what am I missing? Where can I go,
who can I speak with to discover the truth of
hope for myself? Who will bear witness to me?
With what people can I surround myself to
experience this hope in action? If I am hope-

ful, how does this move me to act throughout
my day? When I encounter hurt and broken
people in my life who are without hope, how
do I share the hope and optimism I feel with
them?

Bibliography

Evans, G. Rosemary. *Augustine on Evil*, Cambridge University Press, 1990.

Fitzgerald, Allan D., ed. *Augustine Through the Ages*, Eerdmans, 1999.

Groeschel, Benedict J. *Augustine: Major Writings*, Crossroad NY, 1994.

Hand, Thomas, A. *Augustine on Prayer*, Catholic Book Publishers, 1986.

Hill, Edmund. *The Mystery of God: Saint Augustine on the Trinity*, Harper San Francisco, 1986.

O'Connell, Robert J. *Images of Conversion in Saint Augustine's Confessions*, Fordham University Press, 1995.

____. *Saint Augustine's Confessions: The Odyssey of Soul*, Fordham University Press, 1989.

Price, Richard. *Augustine*, Vardy, Peter, ed. Liguori Publications, 1997.

Saint Augustine. *The City of God*, Doubleday, 1958.

____. *Confessions, Bks. I–IV*, Clarke, Gillian, ed. Cambridge University Press, 1995.

____. *Prayers of Saint Augustine: A Contemporary Anthology*, Harper San Francisco, 1985.

____. *Saint Augustine on the Psalms*, Quasten, J. & Burghardt, Walter J., eds., Paulist Press, 1961.

Sheed, Francis J. *Our Hearts Are Restless: The Prayers of Saint Augustine*, Harper San Francisco, 1984.

Also available in the "15 Days of Prayer" series:

Blessed Frederic Ozanam, Christian Verheyde
    978-1-56548-487-0, paper
    978-1-56548-522-8, ebook
Brother Roger of Taize, Sabine Laplane
    978-1-56548-349-1, paper
    978-1-56548-375-0, ebook
Dietrich Bonhoeffer, Matthieu Arnold
    978-1-56548-311-8, paper
    978-1-56548-344-6, ebook
Henri Nouwen, Robert Waldron
    978-1-56548-324-8, paper
    978-1-56548-384-2, ebook
Jean-Claude Colin, François Drouilly
    978-1-56548-435-1, paper
Saint Benedict, André Gozier
    978-1-56548-304-0, paper
    978-1-56548-340-8, ebook
Saint Bernadette of Lourdes, François Vayne
    978-1-56548-314-9, paper
    978-1-56548-343-9, ebook

Saint Catherine of Siena, Chantal van der Plancke and André Knockaert
    978-1-56548-310-1, paper
    978-1-56548-342-2, ebook
Saint Clare of Assisi, Marie-France Becker
    978-1-56548-371-2, paper
    978-1-56548-405-4, ebook
Saint Elizabeth Ann Seton, Betty Ann McNeil
    978-0764-808418, paper
Saint Eugene de Mazenod, Bernard Duller
    978-1-56548-320-0, paper
Saint Faustina Kowalska, John J. Cleary
    978-1-56548-350-7, paper
    978-1-56548-499-3, ebook
Saint Francis of Assisi, Thaddée Matura
    978-1-56548-315-6, paper
    978-1-56548-341-5, ebook
Saint John of the Cross, Constant Tonnelier
    978-1-56548-427-6, paper
    978-1-56548-458-0, ebook
Saint Teresa of Avila, Jean Abiven
    978-1-56548-366-8, paper
    978-1-56548-399-6, ebook
Saint Thérèse of Lisieux, Constant Tonnelier
    978-1-56548-391-0, paper
    978-1-56548-436-8, ebook
Saint Vincent de Paul, Jean-Pierre Renouard
    978-1-56548-357-6, paper
    978-1-56548-383-5, ebook
Thomas Merton, André Gozier
    978-1-56548-330-9, paper
    978-1-56548-363-7, ebook

NEW CITY PRESS
of the Focolare
Hyde Park, New York

About New City Press of the Focolare

New City Press is one of more than 20 publishing houses sponsored by the Focolare, a movement founded by Chiara Lubich to help bring about the realization of Jesus' prayer: "That all may be one" (John 17:21). In view of that goal, New City Press publishes books and resources that enrich the lives of people and help all to strive toward the unity of the entire human family. We are a member of the Association of Catholic Publishers.

Further Reading

Books by Saint Augustine

The City of God, Books 1-10, 978-1-56548-455-9, $29.95

The City of God, Books 11-22, 978-1-56548-481-8, $39.95

Confessions, Second Ed., 978-1-56548-445-0, $24.95

Trinity, Second Ed., 978-1-56548-446-7, $29.95

Periodicals
Living City Magazine,
www.livingcitymagazine.com

Scan to join our mailing list for discounts and promotions or go to www.newcitypress.com and click on "join our email list."